Dearest

We love you so much!
Happy Valentines Day!

Love,
Mom + Dad.

xoxox

February 2013.

Best Friends Forever

Me and My Dog

A man may smile and bid you hail yet wish you to the devil; but when a good dog wags his tail, you know he's on the level.

Author Unknown

Best
Friends
Forever

Me and My
Dog

What I've Learned
About Life, Love, and Faith
From My Dog

BETHANYHOUSE
MINNEAPOLIS, MINNESOTA

To sit with a dog on a hillside on a glorious afternoon is to be back in Eden, where doing nothing was not boring— it was peace.

Milan Kundera

Contents

Introduction

Dogs have given us their absolute all. We are the center of their universe. We are the focus of their love and faith and trust. They serve us in return for scraps. It is without a doubt the best deal man has ever made.

Roger Caras

There was a time when dogs were wild predators that roamed about the countryside in packs. But one day (who knows why) a dog wandered into or near a human campsite and was offered scraps to eat and allowed to sleep next to a warm fire. He must have been a sharp little guy because he realized right away that this gig was worlds better than running with the pack. All he had to do for his keep was be helpful, entertaining, and pleasant to be around. Thus began the long and mutually rewarding partnership between dog and human.

That alliance is still strong today. The Humane Society estimates that 39 percent of U.S. households have at least one dog. That comes to 74.8 million dogs. And according to the American Kennel Club, there are 150 registered breeds—a dog for almost every purpose, or person, under heaven.

We adore our dogs for many reasons. They are warm, cuddly, happy creatures, loyal and protective, kind and hardworking. They accept us just as we are and love us unconditionally. They connect with us emotionally and teach us without saying a word. For all this, they ask very little, only what they have always asked for: the scraps from our tables and a safe place to sleep.

My parents bought me my first dog when I was just three years old, and since then, I have always had at least one canine companion in my life. Despite the years, I can still call them all by name and describe each one's quirky personality traits. Each was, in his or her own way, unforgettable.

Best Friends Forever: Me and My Dog was inspired by the many dogs that have passed through my life and the lives of other dog lovers who have enthusiastically told me their stories. You will read about dogs that entertain, dogs that heal, dogs that work hard, dogs that fight for our freedom on foreign soil, dogs that survive unbelievable odds, and dogs that give their all for the humans they love.

I invite you to get comfortable with your favorite dog and allow each of these remarkable animals to walk off the pages of this book and into your heart.

He is very imprudent, a dog is. He never
makes it his business to inquire whether
you are in the right or in the wrong,
never bothers as to whether you are
going up or down life's ladder, never
asks whether you are rich or poor,
silly or wise. You are his pal.

✦

Jerome K. Jerome

A Hand Up!

None of us got where we are solely by pulling ourselves up by our bootstraps. We got here because somebody . . . bent down and helped us.

Thurgood Marshall

At some point in life, everyone needs a hand up, help recovering from some unfortunate circumstance, whether the result of one's own poor choices or those of others. Unlike many humans, dogs are happy to take help from others. They appreciate the need for and the joy of being rescued.

Sophie is a rescue dog, though it isn't quite clear if we rescued her or she rescued us. Maybe it was a little of both. Our journey began when some friends told us about an organization called ARF (Animal Rescue Foundation). Their kindhearted volunteers visit the pound looking for dogs they feel are healthy enough to survive and well adjusted enough to be adopted. ARF keeps the dogs until their health can be verified, provides them with shots, tattoos their inner thighs with an identification number, and adopts them out to qualified pet owners. After passing a rigorous competency evaluation (including a home visit), we were approved and waited eagerly for the call that came on a sunny afternoon in August.

Sophie, a blond cocker spaniel/Pekingese mix, burst into the waiting room at the ARF-sponsored animal clinic with her long, fluffy tail wagging. We gave her a good inspection, which wasn't easy with all the jumping and twirling and licking that was going on; clearly she liked us. We noted her large curly ears, big brown eyes, and crooked grin, and we all agreed that she needed a French name. Anita, the ARF volunteer, just shook her head and smiled. She wasn't seeing the French connection, but she was happy to go along. After leaning briefly toward Chéri or Monique, my daughter, Trish, and I settled on Sophie. She seemed to like it—a lot! While the twenty-five-pound two-year-old sniffed our legs and licked our hands, the ARF volunteer filled us in on the circumstances of her rescue.

> *If you pick up a starving dog and make him prosperous, he will not bite you. This is the principal difference between a dog and a man.*
> Mark Twain

Animal control officers had found Sophie wandering in a commercial area of the city. They guessed she had not been homeless long because she was clean and well-nourished and had tested negative for heartworm. There were no obvious signs of injury or abuse, and she was friendly to people. Surely she had been someone's precious pet until some catastrophe put her out on the streets, nameless and alone. When rescued she had no collar or other form of identification, and no one came to ask about her. Animal control had knocked on doors and looked for her mug on missing-dog posters to no avail. Finally, after two months of care and observation, Sophie was ready to be placed with a new family, and we were thrilled to be the chosen ones.

> *You defended me. When I was fenced in, you freed and rescued me because you love me.*
> Psalm 18:18–19 CEV

These days Sophie rules the house. We love her despite her eccentricities. For example, I've never heard a dog make so much noise simply drinking from her water dish. On several occasions, she has gotten away from me and made a beeline for the golf course across the street. Dragging her leash and darting from golfer to golfer, she ran me in circles until some kindhearted soul reached down and snagged her for me. And then there's the fact that Sophie loves to eat grass. She looks it over carefully, nudges it with her paw, and sniffs it first. Clover is her favorite. Her technique might be compared to that of a connoisseur searching out truffles or rare mushrooms, at least in terms of zeal.

We can't imagine our lives without Sophie. She brings a hearty serving of love and laughter to our home every day. Sometimes we see her staring off into space and wonder if she is having a flashback from her life before she came to us. If she is remembering a life now lost to her, she doesn't let it get her down. She just seems glad to have been rescued.

We are all God's helpers. He uses us to help each other, to bless each other, and to love each other. When someone reaches out to help you, that is God at work.
Frances Jean Bechtel

That's one of the big differences between dogs and people. Our four-legged friends have no problem accepting help. They know they are dependent on human beings, and they freely accept whatever is offered. For humans, though, taking a hand up isn't always so easy. We often let pride, fear, and suspicion stand in the way. Sometimes we wonder about ulterior motives or possible strings attached. Even embarrassment can cause us to draw back and linger in our predicament. Sophie wasted no time with these issues. She simply looked up and wagged her tail with gratitude. We should take a lesson.

When we are willing to reach out enthusiastically and receive what is being offered, even situations that seem hopeless often aren't. We can ask God to give us a hand up and out of our circumstances. He may send us a bona fide miracle, but most often he sends caring individuals who long to help.

Far and Away!

The problems of the world cannot possibly be solved by skeptics or cynics whose horizons are limited by the obvious realities. We need men who can dream of things that never were.

John Keats

Most people see only what is right in front of them, while a few refuse to be satisfied with their present surroundings and circumstances. They long to see more. These people can be found gazing into space, focused on what is yet unseen. Such individuals are called visionaries, and occasionally, you may run across a dog like that, though they are ever so rare.

One of those rare creatures lives next door to us. His name is Chewie (short for Chewbacca of *Star Wars* fame). A bundle of rust, black, brown, and red shag, his previous owner called him Walter, though no one can figure out why. By breed, Chewie is a Lhasa Apso. These miniature English sheepdogs are virtual balls of energy.

Chewie's first family purchased him from a breeder as a Christmas gift for one of their children. But when their daughter developed an allergic reaction, they knew they would have to find him a new home. That's how he came to be for sale in a Walmart parking lot one sunny January day. His family had no trouble attracting a crowd, and soon a young college student named Kate happened by. As she hesitated briefly to quell her curiosity, their eyes met, and both the young woman and the bright little pup knew instantly that they were meant for each other. She plopped down the asking price, renamed him Chewie, and carried him back to her university dorm room.

> *A dog, more than any other creature, it seems to me, gets interested in one subject, theme, or object in life, and pursues it with a fixity of purpose which would be inspiring to Man if it weren't so troublesome.*
> E. B. White

Kate and Chewie lived in the dorm until the end of the term. They were good together. They slept side by side on their backs each night with the ceiling fan blowing down on their faces. Each afternoon they shared a cookie Kate saved from her cafeteria lunch. Then Chewie would lie quietly at Kate's feet while she worked on her assignments at the computer—all this with the promise that there would be a walk in it for him if he behaved.

Chewie let his energy and enthusiasm show when he saw the leash come out of the drawer. The walk down the back stairs and outside was more like a run. By the time they hit the sidewalk, the little Lhasa's social instincts were fully alive. He would crisscross the sidewalk in front of her and greet all with the doggy version of a warm handshake. Kate loved it! But it was on their walks that she first noticed another side of Chewie's personality.

At least once during every walk, the frisky little pup would suddenly stop in his tracks and calmly sit down on the sidewalk or a grassy area nearby. No amount of coaxing would get him back to walking until he had satisfied his inner reverie. His dark, deep set eyes would gaze off into the distance at some unseen object far, far away. Kate could not see what Chewie was seeing even though she tried. Perhaps he was searching the distant landscape for his parents and siblings. Or maybe a familiar sound or movement triggered a vision of the adventures he might one day have. When he had seen enough, the rusty little ball of shag would abruptly return to the walk, and Kate felt that Chewie's bounce was a little livelier and his bark slightly more animated. He'd seen something that inspired him, she was sure of that.

> *If people can't see what God is doing, they stumble all over themselves; but when they attend to what he reveals, they are most blessed.*
> Proverbs 29:18 MSG

When Kate left school to take a job in Virginia, she left Chewie with her parents. "He's a dreamer," she told them. "You'll see what I mean." And before long, they did.

These days, Chewie loves to mix it up with Merri Grace and Miss Pip, a Lab and a Yorkie already living in the Baxters' home. They often chase each other around the house and out onto the deck.

They are a lively little group, and Chewie loves to be in the thick of things. But Merri Grace and Miss Pip no longer think a thing about it when the little Lhasa Apso suddenly stops right in the middle of their fun and gazes off into the distance. They have grown used to that faraway look in his eyes, and they know there is little sense in trying to distract him from his vision. It will be over when it's over. Until then, he has something more than doggy play on his mind.

> *Every great dream begins with a dreamer. Always remember, you have within you the strength, the patience, and the passion to reach for the stars to change the world.*
> Harriet Tubman

Like Chewie, we all need to stop occasionally right in the middle of our busy schedules and frenzied activities and just for a few moments stare into the future with the eyes of our hearts. There's more to life than what is right in front of us—much, much more.

Wind and Water

*When . . . it seems as though you could
not hang on a minute longer, never give
up then, for that is just the place and
time that the tide will turn.*

Harriet Beecher Stowe

In just a few hours, everything changed. That's how
many of the residents of New Orleans described Au
gust 29, 2005, as Katrina, a Category 3 hurricane, made
landfall just east of the city. Soon after, the levees broke
and water quickly filled streets, homes, and businesses.
Some people fled, some were rescued, and tragically,
some died. Countless others were forced to leave their
beloved pets behind. It was an unprecedented disaster,
and yet one bedraggled little dachshund proved that a
new beginning is always just beyond the horizon.

The images of those days are seared into the American conscious-
ness: towns devastated all along the Gulf Coast; evacuees stranded
without food, water, and other basic necessities; whole families des-
perately waving from their rooftops. Exhausted rescuers in helicop-
ters and boats spent long days ferrying people to so-called safety in a

crowded sports arena, on highway overpasses, anywhere high ground could be found. The hearts of television viewers broke for the victims and for the many animals left to fend for themselves.

Bess was one of those animals. The black smooth-haired dachshund was stranded on the porch of a house in New Orleans' Ninth Ward. No one knew her name; her family had to go, and they couldn't take her along. Perhaps they thought they would be back in a few days to get her. It's hard to say.

> *Dachshunds are ideal dogs for small children, as they are already stretched and pulled to such a length that the child cannot do much harm one way or the other.*
> Robert Benchley

Almost a week after the storm, two rescue workers, who had noticed the animal on their many passes back and forth ferrying people to safety, stopped and pulled her into their boat. They told animal rescuers, who had assembled to save as many animals as possible, that when they passed anywhere near the little white frame house, they could hear her frantic barking even before they could see her hopping in circles on the small concrete porch. They wondered how she kept going, why she refused to resign herself to the hopelessness around her. She had nipped at their hands as they tried to get her into the boat, but her courage and endurance made it impossible to give up on her.

The two men in the small motorboat gave the rescuers the address where they had found her, thinking the information might help them reunite Bess with her family. But the connection was never made. It's possible her family had simply abandoned their ruined home as so many did. Or they may have found it impossible to come back. Parts of the city, including the Ninth Ward, were off-limits for some time. Many thousands settled in the areas where they had been given refuge, accepting that they really had nothing to go home to. Who could blame them?

> *God saved us from the threat of death, and we are sure that he will do it again and again.*
>
> 2 Corinthians 1:10
> CEV

The rescue workers placed the exhausted dachshund in a crate and loaded her into a transport van. On top of the crate, they taped the information the two men in the boat had provided and the new name she had been given—Bess. From there her journey is sketchy. All that's known for sure is that her crate ended up at a shelter in a small town in Oklahoma. Rescuers cared for her there for another month while her picture and information were posted on an Internet site, but no one called to claim her.

Carol, a writer friend of mine, and her husband, Jay, became Bess's new owners. They were inspired when they read the notes from her rescuers. They admired her spunk. She could have given up, but she didn't; she wouldn't. She kept on barking until it won her a ride out of her predicament. Somehow, she knew there was life to be lived even after the ravages of wind and water, and she fought for that life.

Permanence, persever-ance, and persistence in spite of all obstacles, discouragement, and impossibilities: It is this that in all things distinguishes the strong soul from the weak.
Thomas Carlyle

It takes courage to hold on when the world is crashing down around us. Giving up may even appear logical when our obstacles seem insurmountable. But make no mistake, no matter how dire our circumstances might seem, God has ordained that on this planet the sun comes behind the rain, thaw comes after the freeze, and hope rises from the ashes of disaster.

If sometimes we feel that a Category 3 hurricane has passed through our lives, we should consider this: As long as we are alive, we have the promise of a new beginning. The lives we had might be gone forever, but a new version of life is waiting if we will keep fighting for it. Bess is proof of that.

Check the Manual

Everything in the Scriptures is God's Word. All of it is useful for teaching and helping people and for correcting them and showing them how to live.
2 Timothy 3:16 CEV

Wise dog owners take time to study the characteristics of their pet's specific breed. They want to know what techniques have been used with success to ensure their pet's safety, health, and happiness. The process is made much easier with the help of a manual. God also has a manual, the Bible. In its pages, he gives us the information we need to better know ourselves. When we take it to heart, we learn how to avoid mistakes and live happier, more productive lives.

Miss Pip was born in Florida, one of a litter of miniature Yorkshire terrier pups. The breeder had little trouble finding homes for two of the precious darlings, but the youngest female was reclusive and kept her distance from those who came hoping to take home a puppy. That is, until Vanessa, a stage actress, a dog enthusiast, and our next-door neighbor, happened to be in Florida to perform in a play and was staying at the home of a fellow performer who had two delightful Yorkies of her own. Seeing Vanessa's attraction to the tiny wonders, her host offered to contact the breeder from whom she had acquired her babies.

The initial call was less than encouraging. Only one puppy was left, an undersized female who seemed terrified of everyone. The family had decided she was too fragile to adopt out, but they invited Vanessa and her friend to come by anyway. Perhaps an introduction could be made and a future adoption arranged.

> *God . . . sat down for a moment when the dog was finished in order to watch it . . . and to know that it was good, that nothing was lacking, that it could not have been made better.*
> Rainer Maria Rilke

When the two women arrived, however, the unexpected happened. Miss Pip took one look at Vanessa and begged to get up in her lap. Forget what everyone else had decided, the tiny creature had made her match. The next day, Vanessa placed the Yorkie in a small dog carrier and boarded an airplane back to Oklahoma, christening her Miss Pip even before the plane left the tarmac.

When Vanessa arrived at home with Miss Pip, Vanessa's husband, David, and their two dogs, Merri Grace and Chewie, welcomed the newcomer. She was tiny, barely two pounds, but she soon found her bark and an assertive personality to boot. She was quite literally a "handful."

Warned by the breeder that Yorkies are especially subject to certain inborn maladies, Vanessa made a trip to the bookstore and began a study of the breed. Her little one was a big responsibility, and she wanted to make sure she stayed healthy and happy. In a breeder's manual, she learned that Yorkies have fragile kneecaps. Miss Pip would need to be discouraged from jumping up or jumping down. She was also at

*Show me your paths
and teach me to follow;
guide me by your truth
and instruct me.*
Psalm 25:4–5 CEV

high risk for an abnormal blood flow to the liver. Vanessa studied the symptoms so she would be able to recognize them if Miss Pip had inherited the condition. The manual informed her that her new puppy might also develop a problem with her eyes, and a narrowing of the inner diameter of the trachea was possible.

So far, Miss Pip has shown only a feisty and independent nature, but Vanessa has made it her business to be prepared for any eventuality. Not only has she made herself aware of possible health issues, but she has also learned how best to integrate Miss Pip into the family and cultivate her strengths.

The one who created us, who loves us, and who has adopted us into his family has also written a manual for our benefit. He wants us to be informed so we can make good choices for our-selves physically, emotionally, psychologically, and spiritually. He

warns us about certain behaviors that can lead to trouble as well as behav-iors that can help us lead healthy, hap-py, productive lives. It's all right there in the manual—the Bible.

When you have read the Bible, you will know it is the word of God, because you will have found it the key to your own heart, your own happiness and your duty.
Woodrow Wilson

The Bible often gets a bad rap for its unadorned portrayal of the human condition. But the fact is it simply hits home. It's not always comfortable to address our innate weaknesses, but we are better off knowing the obstacles that may appear in our paths. And the Bible also builds us up, telling us that we are each a unique, deeply beloved member of God's family. It teaches us how to live together in peace while discovering our true potential.

When we sometimes wonder what life is all about and are baffled by our own choices and inclinations, we can pick up God's manual for humans. The more we study it, the more we will see who we were created to be.

Listen, Somebody's Calling

God is always whispering to us, only we do not always hear because of the noise, hurry, and distraction which life causes as it rushes on.

Frederick William Faber

Even the best-behaved dog has been known to head out in search of an adventure—the smell of fresh clover, new people to meet, a warm breeze replete with the promise of bones yet uncovered. When this happens, the only call that pooch is going to hear is the call of the wild. People also have such lapses. It's possible to become so caught up in our busy lives that we wander off and close our ears to the voice of God. But God never gives up; he just keeps calling!

Sophie, our small blond cocker spaniel/Pekingese mix, is usually a docile, obedient dog. While I work at the computer, Sophie lies on a comforter near my feet, watching over her domain with both eyes almost closed and a crooked smile on her face. She pays no attention to the ringing of the phone or the computer's various bells and whistles. The chair moves and creaks with no response.

But all I have to do is whisper her name, and Sophie's tail instantly begins to wag. Sophie is completely tuned in to my voice. That's why it's difficult to believe that the creature bounding across the golf course one sunny spring day was the same dog!

Sophie is allowed only into the fenced backyard without her leash, but on this particular day, a warm breeze blew the inside door to the garage open, and the little pooch suddenly found herself experiencing a fit of spring fever. Since I was busy transferring laundry from the washer to the dryer, I was unaware of Sophie's first tentative steps out into the front yard. By the time I noticed the door standing open and glanced outside, she was happily sniffing clover and bouncing around the front yard. My initial calls from the house were ignored. She didn't even look up. And then, in the brief moment it took me to step into my sandals, Sophie spotted golfers at the golf course across the street and was off and running.

> *"I will search for the lost and bring back the strays. I will bind up the injured and strengthen the weak,"* [declares] the Sovereign LORD.
> Ezekiel 34:16–17 NIV

I called again from the driveway. I was sure I could get her attention and order her back to the house. Boy, was I mistaken. Like a teenager plugged in to an iPod, Sophie followed her nose across the street before stopping to sniff around enthusiastically just on the far side of the fairway. I got there just in time to see her fluffy body disappear over a hill down by the seventeenth tee. She was still ignoring my shouts and whistles.

By the time I reached the place of the last known sighting and came up over the hill, I was huffing and puffing and seriously out of patience. Now I could clearly see Sophie flitting from golfer to golfer without so much as a glance in my direction. She appeared to be all but deaf to my voice, which until that day I had theorized was the center of her universe.

I made it down the hill and within a few feet of snatching her up and snapping on her leash, but Sophie was always just a few steps ahead of me.

> *The voice of God is a friendly voice. No one need fear to listen to it unless he has already made up his mind to resist it.*
>
> A. W. Tozer

Tail wagging vigorously, she greeted every single golfer but paid no attention at all to my frustrated calls and attempts to capture her. The golfers, both amused and embarrassed by my plight, did their best to ignore us both. They kept their eyes down, their mouths shut, and their hands on their putters. Finally, I had had enough. Throwing my arms up in the air, I exclaimed, "Hey, could someone give me a hand here?" At that point, Sophie was busy accosting an older man. With a bemused look on his face, he reached down and snagged her collar, and Sophie's freewheeling vacation came to an abrupt end.

Oh, that you would choose life, so that you and your descendants might live! You can make this choice by loving the LORD your God, obeying him, and committing yourself firmly to him.
Deuteronomy 30:19–20 NLT

It's clear that Sophie loves me. I get that. It's just for a time she became caught up in the adventure of life and tuned out my voice. This often happens with humans, too. No matter how attuned we are to God's voice, there are times when we simply set our faces to the sun and go for it. The thing is, God is *always* calling, *always* pursuing us, though with much more patience and kindheartedness than I showed Sophie that day on the golf course. So here's a tip: If we haven't heard God's voice for a while, maybe we should stop right where we are and listen!

Life Is Short — Relatively Speaking

If we agree that the bottom line of life is happiness, not success, then it makes perfect sense to say that it is the journey that counts, not reaching the destination.
Mihaly Csikszentmihalyi

As a culture, we are age-obsessed. We all start out loving our birthdays, relishing the attention and the celebration. Then at a certain age — thirty, fifty, seventy — the reality of what getting older ultimately means hits us, and we begin to backpedal. Though they probably haven't figured it out, dogs age far more quickly than we do, and yet they don't make a big deal of it. They live their lives to the fullest.

My parents had no children before I was born. In fact, I was the only child for a number of years. It's amazing what parents will do for their firstborn. Every event—bathing, eating, sitting, walking, smiling—is a prime photo op. And oh, how they love to give us things. No expense is spared, no inconvenience too great. When I was three, my parents gave me my very own dog!

Despite my tender age, my mom and dad said it was my duty to name my new pet. I'm told I patted his head and called him Jeff. The name choice must have seemed a bit odd for a three-year-old, but my parents were eager to please, so Jeff it was.

Jeff was a grand dog, a brown and white border collie. He was bright and protective, and I loved him with my whole heart. Though he was not a small animal, he allowed me to dress him up for tea parties, and as I imagined my way through my childhood, he seemed happy to take on whatever role I cared to assign him. We would lie in the grass in the front yard and look for clouds shaped like cows, houses, bathtubs, boats, whatever. I loved this game, though the burden fell on me to do most of the talking.

> *God will prepare every-*
> *thing for our perfect*
> *happiness in heaven,*
> *and if it takes my dog*
> *being there, I believe*
> *he'll be there.*
> Billy Graham

Jeff and I chased butterflies and birds together. He watched attentively as I made mud pies, and he sat beside me during my favorite show, *The Lone Ranger*. He always seemed happy just to be with me.

I taught Jeff a few tricks through the years, but his new abilities didn't go to his head. He seemed to understand his purpose in life was simple—to take care of me.

When I was five, Jeff was hit by a car trying to keep me from marching right into oncoming traffic on a busy highway near our home. Fortunately, he wasn't killed. I ran home to tell my mother, who by that time was frantically searching for me. She cleaned Jeff up, loaded us into the car, and headed for the vet. Jeff recovered quickly, but my parents never let me forget that he had sacrificed his own safety for mine. Without his intervention, I would have been the one with a scarred leg, or worse.

As I entered my teens, Jeff entered retirement. I spent more and more time away from the house, and he spent more and more time

> *I've decided that there's nothing better to do than go ahead and have a good time and get the most we can out of life.*
> **Ecclesiastes 3:12** MSG

lying in the sun. Just the same, he never failed to get up and greet me when I walked up the driveway from school. I'd pat his head, and we'd walk together on into the house.

I was seventeen years old when Jeff died. He was just fourteen. Though I had taken him for granted most of my life, I had a tough time dealing with the loss. Somehow, I imagined he would always be there, just as he always had been. For quite a long time, I cried every day. Coming home in the afternoon was the worst.

All these years later, though, I look back and realize that I wasn't even an official adult when Jeff died, but he was a senior citizen. In dog years, he was very old. Not only that, but he had fulfilled his purpose and enjoyed his life. I was just beginning to consider my life choices, but he had already fulfilled his purpose and enjoyed his retirement. I was just waking up to life, but he was already old and wise.

Carpe diem! Rejoice while you are alive; enjoy the day; live life to the fullest; make the most of what you have. It is later than you think.

Horace

My life will span many more years than Jeff's did. The question is, will I live my life as fully as he lived his? Will I be as certain of my purpose, as determined to do a good job, as willing to do whatever is asked of me? Will those who depend on me find me to be as reliable and as self-sacrificing? Will I spend my golden years lying in the sunshine, greeting the people I love, and dreaming of eternity rather than dreading each birthday? I hope so!

Lost and Found

Let me be aware of the treasure you are. . . . Let me hold you while I may, for it may not always be so.

Mary Jean Irion

For most people, life is a mad dash from the time they get up in the morning until they drop their heads onto their pillows at night. Unfortunately, as our lives rush past us, so do the little joys we receive from those we love. If we're not careful, we lose them. Dogs know how to treat their treasures. They bury them so they can go back later and enjoy them again. What a marvelous idea!

Bosco is all beagle, from his long, wide ears and hazel eyes to his slightly curved, white-tipped tail. Our friends Betty and Herb took one look at his sleek black, brown, and white torso and they were goners. Who could resist that black gumdrop nose? The pleading expression on his face was shouting, "I'm the one for you. Take me home! Please take me home!" And that's exactly what they did. The breeder warned them that beagles can be a bit of a handful, but Bosco's new parents were too busy oohing and aahing to pay much attention. Before they pulled into their driveway, they had named him after Herb's favorite childhood chocolate drink.

Even as a pup, Bosco wasn't much for being held. He was stronger than his new owners expected and way more energetic. He obviously felt snuggling was a big waste of time and greatly preferred sticking his little gumdrop nose into every corner, nook, and cranny. He rooted under every bed and wondered what was behind every door. Clearly, he had a passion for the search.

> *There's a little beagle in all of us —yearning to try something new, searching for an adventure with hope that along the way we can touch a few lives.*
> Dick Wolfsie

Betty and Herb's intention had been to find a quiet, affectionate little house dog, but they quickly realized they had failed miserably in the research department. The question "What were we thinking?" was bandied about on a regular basis. At that point, though, it mattered very little what they had intended. Bosco was now deeply embedded in their hearts. At least he was enthusiastic about everything they did together. Walks on the street were nothing short of an adventure; and the park, now, that was doggy heaven!

Very quickly, Betty and Herb realized that Bosco was by any assessment an outdoor dog. He slept in their room at night on a multicolored blanket they had brought back from a trip to Mexico. But each morning, he made it clear that he was eager to get outside to play in the fenced-in backyard.

It turned out Bosco was a digger, and soon there were holes everywhere. At first, Betty and Herb worried that their precious pooch was trying to make a run for it, but they soon realized he was simply digging for the love of it.

In an effort to save the yard, Bosco's devoted owners presented him with a rawhide bone to gnaw on, but it quickly disappeared without a trace. Disappointed by the loss of the bone, they brought him a chew toy with a bell and a rubber toy. Both were received with a great deal of tail-wagging and high-spirited enthusiasm. And yet a short time later they were missing in action.

> *Don't store up treasures here on earth, where moths eat them and rust destroys them, and where thieves break in and steal. Store your treasures in heaven.*
> Matthew 6:19–20 NLT

My friends wondered if Bosco was hiding his treasures in the yard, and one day that theory was confirmed. As they sunned themselves in their lawn chairs on a beautiful Sunday afternoon, Bosco dropped the rubber toy at Herb's feet. It was clearly intended as a gesture of love. The bright little beagle was hiding his treasures underground, then digging them up when he wanted to play with them or offer them as a demonstration of his true affection. Bosco is a busy dog. He lives his life on the run, but he always has time to guard his treasures.

Let us not get so busy or live so fast that we can't listen to the music of the meadow or the symphony that glorifies the forest. Some things in the world are far more important than wealth; one of them is the ability to enjoy simple things.
Dale Carnegie

As we rush through life, we can't let our treasures get away from us. We need to cherish that tender kiss from our spouse, kind word from a co-worker, hard-won kudos from the boss, handwritten thank-you from our child, sweet face of our newborn grandchild, act of kindness from a stranger, and much-needed word of encouragement from a friend. We need to thank God for each treasure, and then hide it deep in our hearts where we can easily find it later. We never know when we might want to pull our treasures out and remind ourselves what a great life we have.

Dog Behaving Badly

*Man's only legitimate end in life is
to finish God's work — to bring to
full growth the capacities and
talents implanted in us.*

Eric Hoffer

The Bible says that God created each of us with a purpose in mind. Until we discover what that purpose is, we may find ourselves frustrated and unhappy, acting out in ways that bring negative consequences to our lives. Like a cattle dog without cattle, we can languish. But once we are living according to God's plan, we find strength, joy, and contentment.

We were looking for a dog when one of my husband's co-workers produced a snapshot of an adorable black, white, and gray puppy romping in someone's flower bed. "This little guy could sure use a home," she told him. And just that quickly a meeting was arranged. The puppy came and the puppy stayed.

A few days later, on an initial visit to the vet, we learned that our precious little pup was a blue heeler, also known as an Australian cattle dog. That explained the specks of blue in his dense coat. The vet also asked if we happened to have a fenced-in yard, reminding us that puppies don't stay puppies long. "Blue heelers are hardworking, outdoor dogs," he advised us. "They need a lot of exercise and structured activities. They also get pretty big— nineteen to twenty inches tall and thirty to fifty pounds." We were unfazed by this information and unde- terred. We agreed to make it work.

Matching the perfect dog to a specific need not only gives you a beloved pet but a very valuable asset that will enrich your life.
H. Norman Wright

We tossed around a number of names, looking for one that fit just right. At one point, my husband men- tioned that it might help if we could look past the puppy we were holding and try to imagine the dog he would become. Such a pragmatist. But I couldn't seem to get my head or my heart around that no- tion. I stared full into the puppy's eyes and announced that, in the face at least, this dog held a striking resemblance to Humphrey Bogart. Eager to move on, my husband said, "Fine. Then let's call him Bogey."

Unfortunately for our darling blue heeler, we did not have a fenced backyard, only a large concrete deck around the swimming pool. While Bogey was small, he liked playing out there, nosing around in the flower beds that lined the deck and running after squirrels that scampered through. But as time went by and Bogey became the dog God and my husband knew he would be, the owner-dog relationship became tense. We walked Bogey twice a day, once before work and once after work, but those walks just weren't enough. Over time, Bogey became bored, restless, and resentful, and he started acting out.

Bogey chewed on the wooden deck posts and tipped over potted plants. Then he started pulling up strips of the artificial turf that covered part of the deck—and eating it! Though we loved him mightily, it was clear that something had to be done. We remembered what the vet had told us.

> *We always pray for you, asking that our God will make you worthy of his call and will fulfill by his power every good resolve and work of faith.*
> ## 2 Thessalonians 1:11
> NRSV

Bogey was a dog with a purpose, a work dog bred to herd cattle. His doggy nature was conflicted and turning his head toward mischief. We loved him; we forgave him. But it would have been wrong for us to hold on to him for our own selfish reasons.

We asked around and, sure enough, a friend of ours knew someone who was looking for a blue heeler. This mutual acquaintance, a middle-aged man named Darrell, had recently lost his beloved blue heeler in a tragic accident. He owned a small farm with a few cows, horses, and sheep. For the second time in Bogey's life, a meeting was arranged.

Bogey took right to Darrell, and his livestock, as well. He ran from animal to animal, circling them, sizing them up. The little pup was now full-grown, and obviously in his element. It was decided that Bogey would stay with Darrell.

> *We are God's master-piece. He has created us anew in Christ Jesus, so we can do the good things he planned for us long ago.*
> Ephesians 2:10 NLT

Bogey greets us whenever we go to visit. There is much affection on both sides. But even the casual observer can see that the sturdy, confident animal is happy to have a chance to be who God intended him to be.

God has created each of us with a purpose, and we won't be happy until we discover what it is. When we feel angry and frustrated, uncomfortable in our surroundings, we can ask God to help us find out who we were meant to be.

God made the earth, the sky and the water, the moon and the sun. He made man and bird and beast. But he didn't make the dog. He already had one.

Native American Saying

Grass Ball, Anyone?

*A good eater must be a good man;
for a good eater must have a good
digestion, and a good digestion
depends upon a good conscience.*

Benjamin Disraeli

Dogs are incapable of knowing right from wrong on an instinctual basis. All they know is cause and effect, and even then, it's a slow process before they understand the adverse consequences of certain behaviors. We, on the other hand, were given a conscience, an innate connection with purity and goodness. When we err, we feel a twinge inside. But sometimes, like a dog with a bellyache, we rush around trying anything that might ease our discomfort.

Mitzi is a four-year-old black female cocker spaniel and the reigning queen of her castle. My nephew Jason, then twelve, picked her from a litter of pups being sold by a local vet. Getting a dog was Jason's idea from the beginning, and he had already been campaigning hard when he heard the vet had puppies for sale.

As kids have been doing for generations, he bombarded his

parents with promises. He would be responsible for all the dog's maintenance, including feeding, walking, grooming, and training. He assured them that no one else in the family would have to lift a finger. Plus, cocker spaniels are quiet and practically no trouble at all. He'd be surprised if they even noticed there was a dog in the house, especially after he finished training it to be the best, most well-behaved dog that ever lived.

Finally, Jason convinced my sister Anne to go down to the vet's office and just take a look. It turned out to be a clever strategic move. What person alive could resist that gorgeous

> *You bite open plastic jar of peanut butter, eat entire contents. Delicious now. But making pig of self is not beautiful. So, later feel shame. And have big intestinal-tract distress.*
>
> Trixie Koontz, dog in *Bliss to You: Trixie's Guide to a Happy Life*

coat and regal head? The large curly ears and big brown eyes could easily steal your heart away. The fluffy little fur ball all but threw herself into Jason's arms, and that was all it took. Since the little female was the only pup left, the vet asked a hundred dollars, about one-fifth of the usual price. It was almost every cent Jason had saved, but he handed it right over, and mother and son took the happy little creature home.

At first, Jason was diligent about his promises, and he and Mitzi (a name suggested by Jason's sister, Emma) were always together.

He kept her food and water bowls full and walked her both before and after school. On Saturdays he would brush her thick, black coat and teach her to obey a few commands like sit, stay, and come. But as Jason got busy with sports and other interests, Mitzi became a family pet.

> *I have the same hope in God that these men have, that he will raise both the righteous and the unrighteous. Because of this, I always try to maintain a clear conscience before God and all people.*
> Acts 24:15–16 NLT

Jason's dad, Nick, didn't have much time for upkeep, but he always found time to pull Mitzi's big floppy ears up over her eyes and say, "Guess who?" Emma, five years younger than Jason, eventually took over the food and water duties, and the rest fell to Mom.

The truth was they all adored her. Emma liked to lay her head on Mitzi's back while she watched TV, and one day the kids came home from school to see Mitzi decked out in green and red ribbons and Anne snapping photos for the yearly Christmas card, which has featured only Mitzi ever since.

Now, Mitzi may sound like the perfect animal, and she almost is. There was puppy stuff at first—chewed sneakers, a few accidents on the carpet, the incessant harassment of any guest who walked through the door.

But four years later, the cocker spaniel has outgrown most of her puppy shenanigans. Only one big problem remains. Mitzi has a weakness for eating things she shouldn't. Popcorn, potato chips, half a granola bar, a bologna sandwich . . . whatever has been carelessly left within her reach. Inevitably, a few hours after her culinary indiscretion, Mitzi will beg to be let out into the backyard, where she will eat grass until she upchucks a huge grass ball and the contents of her soured stomach. Poor Mitzi still hasn't connected the dots between poor food choices and bellyaches. That's a dog's life.

> *Let us draw near to God with a sincere heart in full assurance of faith, having our hearts sprinkled to cleanse us from a guilty conscience.*
> Hebrews 10:22 NIV

When we humans do things we shouldn't, we usually get a heartache rather than a bellyache. Often we try to get rid of it by distracting ourselves with activities and possessions, making excuses, or blaming others. But we are children of God, created in his image. He has given us the capacity to learn from our mistakes and the relief of knowing that our discomfort will end when we say we're sorry and hear God say, "You are forgiven."

Doggy in the Hood

Twenty years from now you will be more disappointed by the things that you didn't do than by the ones you did do. So throw off the bowlines. . . . Explore. Dream. Discover.

Mark Twain

Safety is a big issue in our world, hence the extensive use of dead bolts, passwords, video cameras, car alarms, security systems, and of course, the ever-popular guard dog. All these items have one thing in common, however. They guard indiscriminately. They lock out everyone and everything. It's one thing to be safe, another to be isolated. We must use the tools we've been given, including our God-given ability to keep our hearts and lives open to the world around us.

Soda is one smart dog, that's for sure. Our daughter, son-in-law, and their two boys are convinced that if she were human, she'd have won thousands of dollars by now on *Jeopardy* or *Who Wants to Be a Millionaire*. And amazingly, she isn't just smart. She also has a heightened sense of hearing and smell, and she can detect movement from a great distance. They swear she can hear a pin drop in the next county and see a car pull into a driveway six blocks away. Add to that her exceptional speed and agility, and we have to ask where she keeps her cape and spandex bodysuit with the big S on the front.

This incredible dog is a tricolored (black, white, and brown) border collie. She loves her family, and they certainly love her. Our grandsons Dustin and Jonathan named her Soda, and when I asked why, they looked at me strangely and explained that Soda is short for Soda Pop, which, in my mind at least, doesn't exactly clear up the mystery.

We got a dog for safety reasons, that seeming to be a better option than a handgun. Unfortunately, the animal never met a stranger she didn't like. It's the vacuum cleaner she finds menacing.

Jeremy Bechtel

Border collies are a working breed. Their speed, agility, and intelligence are perfect for herding sheep and cattle, but Soda lives in the suburbs, so she invests her skills wherever she can find a place for them. Most often that means patrolling the perimeter of the backyard from fence post to fence post. She takes her work seriously. No bunny, bird, lizard, or squirrel comes near without her inspection. This is, of course, always accompanied by a loud and nerve-shattering spell of barking that clearly says to her people inside, "Don't worry. Stay calm. I've got this!"

Soda is hypervigilant indoors as well. She goes from window to window, door to door, listening intently and doing her best to continue her comprehensive protection plan.

Now, it should be clearly understood that Soda is not a menacing animal. Her bark and behavior are not in any way predatory. They are intended only to sound the alarm and ensure the safety of her people. Trish says, "Watch out. She disarms her victims by barking them into a state of unconsciousness. Then she takes a run at them and gives them a brutal tongue-licking!"

> *Pray for us . . . that we may be rescued from wicked and evil people; for not all have faith. But the Lord is faithful; he will strengthen you and guard you from the evil one.*
> 2 Thessalonians 3:1–3
> NRSV

Soda also does not bother to evaluate the severity of the danger afoot. She barks at the mail carrier, the neighbors, visitors, passersby, and of course, other dogs (even familiar ones). She barks at anyone and everyone, including David, Trish, and the boys. If there's a difference between her danger bark and her greeting bark, no one has figured it out yet. David and Trish often say to each other, "The good news is, we don't have to worry about someone sneaking in and killing us all in our sleep!"

Although she drives them crazy at times, Soda's family is glad to have her on the job. An expensive motion detector covering their entire property wouldn't be nearly as effective. They just wish they could teach her to discriminate between unwelcome intruders and welcome guests, a poisonous snake and a harmless bunny. As smart as she is, Soda doesn't have the capacity to distinguish a real threat from a perceived one.

Sometimes people have this same problem. We look around at the endless number of threats, both real and imagined, and decide to fortify the boundaries of our homes and our hearts. The vigilance is admirable, but the administration is severe. In the process of guarding ourselves, we cut ourselves off from life.

> *The LORD is my light and my salvation; whom shall I fear? The LORD is the stronghold of my life; of whom shall I be afraid?*
> Psalm 27:1 NRSV

God says repeatedly in the Bible that he does not want us to live in fear or isolate ourselves from one another. His plan is for us to live life to the fullest. That means we may have to prayerfully stick our toes into the water, or take a well-calculated risk. Safety is a good thing, but it isn't everything.

Oh, to Be Near You

Humble yourselves before God. Resist the devil, and he will flee from you. Come close to God, and God will come close to you.

James 4:7–8 NLT

Dogs vary drastically by breed. A St. Bernard and a Chihuahua, for example, would seem to have very little in common. One characteristic, however, is shared by almost every breed, regardless of size, age, color, or temperament: devotion to their masters, despite the fact that in most cases the dogs have no say in who that might be. Unlike our dog friends, we have the privilege of choosing whom we will serve. If we choose God, we should demonstrate our devotion even more enthusiastically.

At first take, Holly would seem an unlikely name for a Siberian husky. Of course, seeing the little black-and-white ball of fur playing with the discarded bows from the Christmas morning revelry might add a touch of understanding. A few hours earlier, she had been wearing one of those bows. She was the best Christmas gift Daniel had ever received, or so he kept announcing repeatedly to absolutely anyone who would listen.

Finally, nine-year-old Daniel curled up on the sofa and fell asleep. He'd been awake half the night hoping for a puppy and awake since five trying to persuade his parents to let him check under the tree. Of course, when they finally relented around seven-thirty, he flew down the stairs only to find plenty of beautifully wrapped packages, but no puppy.

Disappointment was written all over his face. But he quickly turned jubilant when his parents brought the little guy in from the garage a couple of hours later. Boy and dog romped around the living room and then the garage, once the noise level became too much for Daniel's mom. They ended up in the snow-covered front yard where, except for her black nose, perky black-and-white ears, and red bow, Holly would have disappeared altogether. By noon, it was clear Daniel was no match for her boundless energy.

> *Our dogs, like our shoes, are comfortable. They might be a bit out of shape and a little worn around the edges, but they fit well.*
> Bonnie Wilcox

That was how it all began. Eleven years have passed since that Christmas morning. My nephew Daniel is away at the University of Michigan working on a degree in mechanical engineering. In the meantime, Holly has become his parents' dog. The little puppy is now a full sixty pounds. Peg is fond of telling visitors, "We like to think of Holly as not a dog but more of a smallish cow." And if you saw her from a distance, you might agree, since her ample girth is covered by her fluffy white coat with large black spots.

Holly is still amazingly playful for her age and size. But now in her golden years, her favorite thing to do is to lie on the floor next to Peg, or Daniel's father, Roland. Actually, it would be more accurate to say she lies down on them. She just can't seem to get close enough, so she positions herself right on top of their feet and then drops off into a comfortable slumber. When Daniel comes home for the weekend, Holly runs around in a circle—her traditional "happy" dance—but as soon as he puts his stuff away and settles down on the sofa, she lies down on top of his sneakers and nods off.

> *You're all I want in heaven! You're all I want on earth! When my skin sags and my bones get brittle, GOD is rock-firm and faithful.*
> Psalm 73:25–26 MSG

Holly greets all the Martins' guests enthusiastically. She is gentle and friendly and likes to make strangers, young and old alike, feel welcome. She enjoys being in the room when people are talking and laughing and having fun. She's a big sweetheart of a dog. But lying down on their feet? Well, that's reserved for the very special people in her life, those she is uncompromisingly devoted to. Only with Daniel, Peg, and Roland does she demonstrate that she adores them so much she simply can't get close enough. And it's obvious that they adore her as well. Holly's naps tend to run long these days, but they wouldn't think of disturbing her. So they sit with their feet pinned to the floor until the old husky wakes up and sets them free.

When it comes to God, how devoted are we? Do we love being in his presence? Some people go to church in order to feel close to God. But those of us who are most devoted to him are like Holly. We can't get close enough. We aren't satisfied with an

Nearer, my God, to thee, nearer to thee! E'en though it be a cross that raises me, still all my song shall be, nearer, my God, to thee; nearer to thee!
Sarah F. Adams

arm's-length relationship. We want to move in closer and closer until we are there at his feet, touching him, feeling his warmth, gathering life, strength, and spiritual energy. The Bible assures us that God invites this level of closeness from those who have true, faithful, and devoted hearts.

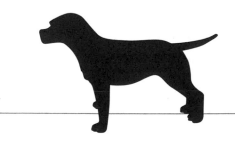

Altogether Different

We have become not a melting pot but a beautiful mosaic. Different people, different beliefs, different yearnings, different hopes, different dreams.

Jimmy Carter

Though there's probably no way to prove it conclusively, traditional wisdom states that no two snowflakes are identical. The same is true of leaves, trees, seashells, and flowers. No two dogs are alike, and if you've ever spent time sitting in an airport, you know that no two people are alike, either. Clearly, God could have filled the world with simple uniformity, but he preferred to make each person, animal, and thing special and beautiful in its own way.

Though it isn't one of the more familiar breeds, the Basenji is a small, athletic dog about the size of a fox terrier. Ears straight and open in the front, small, almond-shaped eyes, and a wrinkly furrowed brow quickly tell any observer that this dog was cut from a different mold. Its distinctive gait is more that of a horse than a dog. But wait, there's more. This wonderfully unique animal does not bark—at all. Instead, it yodels, howls, growls, or crows, depending on how it is feeling at the moment.

The Mudi dog is another uncommon breed, and the owners of these dogs say they are uncommonly remarkable. They are friendly, hardworking herders, with wedge-shaped heads and pointed noses, dark brown, oval eyes, and ears that stand upright in the shape of upside-down Vs. They are medium in height and weight with wide-set back legs. No one knows why, but they are often born without tails. Their coats are long, dense, and wavy. The most

> *Walking two dogs is a little like flying a kite with each arm. At first it seems impossible, but eventually you learn to anticipate the wayward directions each line might take.*
> Ken Foster

unusual thing about the Mudi, though, is the potentially limitless colors of their coats. These dogs can be black, white, red, brown, gray, bread-pale, or fallow. A few come in blue-merle, a striking color made up of black spots of various sizes on a gray background. The grays vary from light silver to dark smoke. The spots can be small specks, very large patches, or an interesting combination of both. God must have used the big sixty-four-count box of crayons when he worked on these fabulous dogs.

The Chinese crested dog comes in two varieties: hairless and powder-puff. The hairless is truly unique. Its soft, humanlike skin is accented by tufts of hair on its paws and tail and long, flowing hair on its head. These fascinating animals often sport a beard. They are also subject to sunburn, so their owners must apply baby sunscreen before they spend time in the sun. In 2003, a Chinese crested named Sam won the competition for the World's Ugliest Dog.

What a wildly wonderful world, GOD! You made it all, with Wisdom at your side, made earth overflow with your wonderful creations.
Psalm 104:24 MSG

The Shar-Pei spends the first few years of its life growing into its own skin. Deeply wrinkled with a blue-black mouth, these dogs will not be confused for any other breed. They have three types of distinctive coats: One feels like horsehair, rough and prickly to the touch; a second is long and smooth; and a third variety has an undercoat. Tiny ears that fall forward and a tail carried in a curl declare that this dog is like no other.

There is a long list of unusual dogs, such as the bloodhound and the dachshund. And there are rare dogs like the Sloughi, the Lowchen, and the puli. But every dog, even those from common breeds, have their own distinct characteristics, personalities, and temperaments—as any dog owner will be quick to point out. Just like snowflakes, trees, and spider webs, no two dogs are exactly alike.

No two people are exactly alike, either. Each one of us came off God's pottery wheel as a one-of-a-kind original. God didn't break the mold; there never was one.

There is within our human nature a tendency to fear or distrust anyone who is not like us. It's clear that God is the author of differences in his creation. He created them, and then the Bible says he looked and said, "It is good."

God could have made us cookie-cutter copies, but he wanted to look

[People] may be said to resemble not the bricks of which a house is built, but the pieces of a picture puzzle, each differing in shape, but matching the rest, and thus bringing out the picture.
Felix Adler

into each face and see someone special, someone memorable, someone unique. Knowing that God created our differences should change forever the way we think about the issues of color and ethnicity. Not only should we embrace our differences, but we should also celebrate them.

The Call of the Wild

All of us, like sheep, have strayed away. We have left God's paths to follow our own. Yet the Lord laid on him the sins of us all.

Isaiah 53:6 NLT

Some experts estimate that our furry, four-legged friends have been domesticated for thousands of years, but the instinct to run free is still deeply embedded in their DNA. Our human story is somewhat similar. We were wild and undisciplined, runners from the truth, when God brought us into his family. We are now his dear children, and yet each day we must deal with our old human nature that urges us to run after forbidden pleasures.

When we look at our beloved dogs with their jaunty gaits, eager-to-please faces, and beseeching eyes, it's difficult to believe their ancestors were wild animals, roaming free, killing for food, and leading unruly, predatory lives. We place smart-looking collars around their necks and teach them to fetch sticks and Frisbees. We do our best to forget. And with most dogs, we succeed. The joy of being someone's beloved pet outweighs the call of the wild. But occasionally we fall in love with a dog that yearns to wander.

Our wonderful little mutt Missy had just passed away from a stroke. She came to us as a stray and lived with us for more than ten years, so we were heartbroken but not altogether surprised when we lost her. We gathered the children together and buried her with loving care in a secluded area on the south side of the house. A few weeks later we were ready to look for another dog.

Our weaknesses are like dogs, you see. If we walk toward them, they will run away from us. But if we run away from them they'll chase us.
Hugh Nibley

On our first trip to the animal shelter, we were introduced to Brittany, an attractive Irish Setter mix. She was in remarkable shape for a stray, but all attempts to reunite her with her previous owners had failed, and she was deemed adoptable. Brittany was a lovely shade of mahogany, and her long, silky coat was one bath and brushing away from being gorgeous. She took to us right away, especially to the children, and seemed enthusiastic about going home with us.

Brittany was given the run of the house and the backyard. We also took her on long walks up and down our dead-end street. We did take her once to visit some relatives who lived in a rural area with the idea that she could be off the leash for the day, but we quickly discovered she had no sense of boundaries. Once off the leash, she disappeared, and it took us hours to find her.

Back home, Brittany never seemed to be content, though we treated her like a queen. Early on, she escaped from the backyard and made a run for it. Fortunately, the information on her collar brought her back to us. We reinforced the fence in the back, which kept her enclosed until someone let her inside the house. Once there she would wait until an unsuspecting family member or guest opened the front door, and then she would push her way past them and set off at a dead run. I wondered if my last image of her would be her beautiful silky coat flying in the wind as she dashed out of sight. At least twice a week we had to mount a search and bring her home.

> *Let the wicked change their ways and banish the very thought of doing wrong. Let them turn to the LORD that he may have mercy on them. Yes, turn to our God, for he will forgive generously.*
> Isaiah 55:7 NLT

After a few months it became obvious that our relationship with Brittany was not working out. She was a sweet dog, never aggressive or snappish. The children loved her and so did we, but spending so much time chasing her down had created an untenable situation. At first, we were hurt that she seemed to be obsessed with getting away from us. But ultimately we realized that Brittany loved us, but she just had a heart that longed to wander. Unwilling to chain or cage her, we were left with no alternative. We took her to the Animal Rescue Foundation for adoption to a more appropriate home.

Human beings have always employed an enormous variety of clever devices for running away from themselves, and the modern world is particularly rich in such stratagems.

Josh Billings

There is a "call of the wild" within our human natures, as well. Though we have been adopted by God and shown great love, we still have a tendency to run away from responsibility, run away from the truth, run away from what we know is best for us. But unlike Brittany, we humans have been given the power to resist temptation, the power to choose to stay rather than run. And when we do stray, we can come back home, knowing God has chosen to forgive us.

Pack Mentality

Don't copy the behavior and customs of this world, but let God transform you into a new person by changing the way you think.

Romans 12:2 NLT

Dogs are pack animals; they are social by nature. They stick together, and if given the opportunity, they get into mischief together. One dog alone is apt to be polite and well behaved, but add a second or a third to the mix, and otherwise perfect pets can become a destructive mob. This is often true for humans, as well. We tend to emulate those with whom we keep company.

Dogs just like to have fun, and Sage and Clemie are proof positive of that. These yellow American Labrador retrievers are sisters born from the same mother a year apart. Robert, their owner, says Sage, the older of the two, was feisty as a pup. She once chewed up his tennis shoe and unsuccessfully attempted to dig out under the back fence. But overall, she was a good dog. It was normal for her to fetch a stick or two or wrestle around on the ground, maybe even dig up a bone and place it at Robert's feet. If anything, though, she may have been a little too docile.

That's why Robert thought she might need a companion. He was thrilled to hear that Sage's mother had just had a litter of pups. One of the females was still available, and the breeder promised to call as soon as she was weaned. Sage wasn't sure what to do with her at first, but she quickly took a liking to her little sister. Robert named her Clementine (Clemie for short). The adorable little puppy gave Sage a new lease on life.

> *Most dogs are intimidated by bears, but in the presence of other dogs their pack mentality kicks in and they may give chase. Chasing a bear is not a good thing!*
> Beth Fowler

Then one day Robert got a call at work from a neighbor, who reported seeing Sage and Clemie roughhousing on someone else's front lawn. When he pulled into the driveway, his two recalcitrant pets met him at the car. They stood with guilty faces as he examined the pile of dirt and the hole under the fence. Robert shored up the hole and placed some boards over the soft ground. But a few days later, their remorse forgotten, they escaped again by way of a hole under the front gate.

The first time the dogs made their way to freedom, they

seemed surprised to have actually pulled off a successful escape. But this time their boldness must have been intoxicating. There are no human witnesses to what happened after that, except that a woman who lives a few houses down said she saw them running back and forth through the neighborhood earlier in the day. The physical evidence, however, did a good job of documenting the dogs' crime spree. One neighbor's trash can was tipped over and the trash tracked around the side yard; and the man across the street reported several potted plants were toppled over and doggy paw prints could be seen in the newly planted flower bed. The worst of it, though, took place two houses down on the left.

Mob Mentality: In sociology, this is a group of persons stimulating one another to excitement and losing ordinary rational control over their activity.
Verilese Graeme

After several rainy, overcast days, the sun was actually shining, so neighbor Charlotte had decided to sit at her picnic table and fold laundry. "I just went inside for a minute," she later reported to Robert, "just long enough to answer the phone and put another load in the washer." When she came back out, she saw Sage and Clemie and an unidentified perpetrator, described by Charlotte only as "big and brown," playing tug-of-war with one of her good bath towels. The rest of the laundry was strewn about the yard. Her coffee cup was lying in the grass, and all that was left of her partially eaten bran muffin was a torn paper baking cup.

Robert would say that Sage and Clemie aren't really bad dogs. In fact, most of the time they are model citizens. He thinks of them more as two honor students who decided to skip school on senior day and got caught up in some unfortunate incident. A little sunshine, a random act of rebellion, and bad company can add up to disaster.

> *There's trouble ahead when you live only for the approval of others. . . . Your task is to be true, not popular.*
> Luke 6:26 MSG

It's easy for humans to get into trouble in much the same way. We are sometimes willing to do things in a group that we would never do alone. Things like gossip, racial slurs, intimidation, for example. Let's take a lesson from Sage and Clemie's disastrous day and take care not to be caught up in pack mentality.

Never Too Old to Play

I think you should be a child for as long as you can. I have been successful for 74 years being able to do that. Don't rush into adulthood, it isn't all that much fun.

Bob Newhart

Children and puppies live to play and have all the energy and enthusiasm they need to do it well. But as adults, we allow the responsibilities and concerns of life to creep in and steal our fun. And with the loss of our fun, we lose some of our joy over the miracle of being alive. We could take a lesson from Jesse, who found time for play long into his golden years.

Jesse was born in my grandfather's barn. His mother, Cleo, was part German shepherd and part mystery dog, and his father was thought to be an Australian cattle dog from a neighboring farm. My dad was nine when the puppies were born, and my grandfather gave him the responsibility of caring for Cleo and her pups. He checked on them several times a day and in the process grew attached to one of the three males in the litter. Two weeks after the puppies were born, my dad asked Grandpa if he could keep the black one with the white spot above his left eye.

Grandfather agreed but insisted on the following conditions: My dad was not to take the puppy too far from the litter until he was weaned. He was to feed him only what the other dogs were eating. He was not allowed to take him into the house. And he was to remember that this was a working dog, expected to earn his keep just like the others. Dad agreed.

No one is sure where my dad came up with the name Jesse. When I asked before writing this story, my dad claimed he couldn't remember, and my mom said it was probably after Jesse James, the bank robber. She delivered this line with a wink in my father's direction and the trace of a smirk on her lips. I'm guessing that somewhere in there is a private joke I'll never be privy to.

> *The dog has got more fun out of Man than Man has got out of the dog, for the clearly demonstrable reason that Man is the more laughable of the two animals.*
>
> James Thurber

Dad says Jesse always met him at the top of the driveway when he stepped off the school bus. Dad would put his books on the porch, and for the next hour the two would engage in any number of games—chase, fetch, tug-of-war, and hide-and-seek. They also chased butterflies and birds and raced back and forth between the barn and the house (a game Dad says he never once won). My dad instilled in Jesse a love for play that he held on to throughout his long life.

My dad was called up for military service at the age of eighteen. It was near the end of World War II, which meant he missed the worst of the fighting, but he spent two years in Italy repairing airplanes. When he came home, he married my mom, his high school sweetheart, and they moved to Gary, Indiana, where my father got a job in a steel mill. I was born a little more than a year later.

All you who fear GOD, how blessed you are! how happily you walk on his smooth straight road! You worked hard and deserve all you've got coming. Enjoy the blessing! Revel in the goodness!
Psalm 128:1–2 MSG

We visited Grandpa and Grandma as often as we could. Dad says he would honk as the car turned into the driveway, and old Jesse would get up from his place just to the left of the porch steps and greet us with tail wagging. Dad said how amazed he was that the old dog would always bring a stick and drop it at his feet. Dad would throw the stick and then wrestle with him in the grass before we even went inside.

I was only a few years old at the time, but I remember the old black dog with the white spot above his eye. Jesse was seventeen years old when he died. My dad says old Jesse never lost his desire to play.

I wonder if play was the secret of Jesse's long life. He worked hard but then gave himself up to the delights of chasing sticks, twirling in circles, and rolling in the grass. It's an interesting thought for those of us who think we are too old to play. Perhaps play is actually what we need to keep us from feeling old. There's something invigorating in the

I came so that everyone would have life, and have it in its fullest.
John 10:10 CEV

act of overruling our aches and pains and the weight of life's burdens and becoming carefree playmates just for a while, just for the fun of it. Who says old people can't learn new tricks!

Water Dogs

*Things have come to a pretty pass,
our romance is growing flat, for
you like this and the other, while
I go for this and that.*
Ira Gershwin

Have you ever watched someone bungee off the top of a bridge and asked yourself, "Why in the name of all things safe and sane would anyone do that?" That's the way things go in life. What one person considers fun, another person often thinks of as pure, unadulterated terror. We will never completely understand one another, but we can find it in our hearts to be generous and tolerant just the same.

Sage and Clemie, the yellow Labrador retrievers born a year apart from the same mother, are truly a gang of two, playing together, getting into mischief together, and enjoying a good swim together. Because they are bred from American stock, these solid, muscular dogs are taller and lankier than their English counterparts. Slightly taller than they are long, with strong, muscular bodies, Sage and Clemie truly dominate their home turf.

Clemie was just six weeks old when Robert brought her home to Sage. The older dog stepped up immediately and began to protect and train the youngster as if she were her own offspring. Now that Clemie is grown, the two look after each other, with the exception that Clemie always gives Sage, the alpha dog, a wide berth at the food dish.

Bubbling over with energy, Sage and Clemie seem to be in constant motion, playing tug-of-war with a dish towel someone left on the picnic table, rooting around the mouth of a small hole they've discovered, and periodically checking the periphery of the yard for any signs of a lurking intruder. But the real fun comes when Robert hooks up the hose and the water wars begin.

Poodles are the fashionistas of the dog world, setting the standard for fashionable and chic. A pit bull, on the other hand, would rather dig a hole in the backyard than attend a red carpet event.
Shirleen Kreger

Sage and Clemie are so in tune with this game that they stop in their tracks when Robert steps out into the backyard. He might have come out for any number of reasons, but it's clear that water is the first thing on Sage's and Clemie's minds. They stand stock-still until Robert's purpose becomes apparent. If it seems he might be heading for the hose, they begin to react with quivering muscles, wagging tails, and low-pitched yips. And the second Robert reaches for the hose, they explode with excitement.

The Labs are crazy-wild about water. They run full into it, jump up to meet it, twirl around in it as it snakes out the hose. Their enthusiasm is wonderful to watch. A couple of times a month during warm weather, Robert takes Sage and Clemie to a nearby park that has a small lake at one end. The dogs think it's heaven.

> *There are different kinds of gifts, but the same Spirit. There are different kinds of service, but the same Lord. There are different kinds of working, but the same God works all of them in all men.*
> 1 Corinthians 12:4–6
> NIV

Just down the street, Sophie, the cocker spaniel/Pekingese mix you know from earlier stories, treats the water as if it might be brimming with dog-eating sharks. She will have none of it. She, too, likes to go to the park—the same one Sage and Clemie go to—but while the Labs are splashing their way along the sandy shoreline and submerging their lean bodies in the shallow water, Sophie pretends the lake doesn't exist.

It could be that the Labs are more comfortable with water because of their short, water-resistant double coats, while cocker spaniels have all that long, curly hair to think about. Some owners speculate that cockers resist the water because their long, floppy ears are subject to infection. Whatever it is, Sophie has her reasons.

Like dogs, people are distinctly different in the way they perceive certain elements of life around them. Some people love to rough it, getting back to nature, sleeping under the stars, while others believe the only acceptable campout is a reasonably priced hotel chain. Some like speed; others take it slow and easy.

God has given us different gifts for doing certain things well. So if God has given you the ability to prophesy, speak out with as much faith as God has given you.
Romans 12:6 NLT

Clearly, God fashioned us differently, and he gave us options. What would the world look like if we all had a passion for the same things? It would be a terribly unbalanced world for sure. So if our best friend loves the sun and we don't, we can revel in that. Different is good!

He wa'n't no common dog, he wa'n't no
mongrel; he was a composite. A composite
dog is a dog that is made up of all the
valuable qualities that's in the dog
breed—kind of a syndicate; and a mongrel
is made up of all riffraff that's left over.

Mark Twain

The Power of Perky Persistence

Most of the important things in the world have been accomplished by people who have kept on trying when there seemed to be no hope at all.
Dale Carnegie

Too often we miss out on good things because we give up too soon. We tell ourselves that it's no use, we won't win, nothing ever works out, and we don't have what it takes. Getting what we want is within our reach, but we let it slip through our fingers. One little dog saw something she wanted and was determined to make it her own.

Making guesses about Missy's ancestry was a regular amusement in our family. She was a smallish dog with a long shaggy coat, mostly brown and gray. She looked something like a Lhasa Apso, but the face and tail were all wrong.

She just appeared on the street one spring day, stopping at this house or that, taking any friendly handout. When she reached our house at the end of the block, she must have liked what she saw because, like a true squatter, she found a comfortable, shaded spot on our front lawn and settled her-self down—for good. Calm and unpretentious, she never jumped up or demanded our attention. Instead, she would perk up when someone came outside, put on her best doggy smile, wag her tail in greeting, and follow us at a courteous distance until we disappeared back indoors.

Our four elementary-age children were quickly enamored of the shaggy little stray. After a few days, we gave them permission to pet her, but not to feed her. Honestly, we thought she'd move on when she got hungry enough, but she never did. Two days turned into two weeks, and the little squatter stayed put. Still I refused the children's frequent requests to feed "Little Missy" just "one little cookie" or "one little piece of bread."

> *Perhaps nothing can wrench the heart of a dog lover more than the pitiful, hardly daring-to-be-hopeful gaze of an abandoned dog waiting to be adopted.*
> John Galsworthy

The neighbors had all grown fond of her as well. They frequently promoted her case by remarking, "That little dog sure seems to like your family. Don't you think you ought to keep her?" My standard response was, "No way. We have four children; the last thing we need is a dog." But along about week three, I began to waffle. She was gentle with the children and well behaved. It was getting tougher and tougher to look down at that oddly shaped face and those beseeching eyes. Besides, I was beginning to worry that she might simply starve to death right there on the front lawn.

I know now that several neighbors had been feeding her on the sly, but at the time, all we saw was a sweet little animal so longing to be part of our clan that she was staging a hunger strike right outside our front door.

What a gift life is to those who stay the course! You've heard, of course, of Job's staying power, and you know how God brought it all together for him at the end. That's because God cares.

James 5:11 MSG

Two days into week three, I finally gave in. After dropping the kids off at school, I scooped up Little Missy (the name the kids had given her) and took her to the vet. He gave her a thorough examination, administered her shots, and then gave me the bad news.

"You're kind to try to rescue this little dog," he told me. "But unfortunately, she has a bad case of heartworm, and the only treatment is expensive and unreliable. Don't get too attached because you won't have her long, a year at the most."

That afternoon I had the boys give her a bath in their kiddie pool, and after she dried out, we brought her inside for the first time. We put out food and water bowls, and formally welcomed her. Little Missy settled into our home as if she'd been born there.

The interesting thing is that Little Missy lived with us not one but ten years—that's right, ten! We took her to the vet each year,

Keep on being brave! It will bring you great rewards. Hebrews 10:35 CEV

and each year he told us her time was short. But the heartworm never got her. In the end, she succumbed to a stroke.

Think of all the things we miss in life because we aren't determined enough to keep waiting for them, to keep believing for them. We give up too easily. Little Missy never gave up on the idea of making us her family. And she wasn't about to give up on her life, either, certainly not because some doctor said so. She lived and loved on her own terms. What a wonderful way to celebrate life.

Fear and Trembling

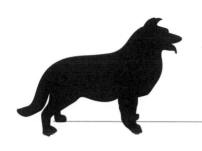

*All of us are born with a set of
instinctive fears —falling, the dark,
lobsters, falling on lobsters in the dark,
speaking before a Rotary Club, or the
words "Some Assembly Required."*
Dave Barry

Fear is a natural part of the human condition. It keeps us from obvious dangers such as playing with fire and crossing the freeway on foot. Fear was designed to be a tool, part of our arsenal of survival resources. But if we aren't watchful, fear can take over our lives and leave us too frightened to enjoy the good things God has given us. As one little Chihuahua would tell you, that's no way to live.

The five-pound Chihuahua is actually three years old, but it's easy to think of him as forever a pup since he fits so sweetly into one's hands. He has all the physical characteristics one would expect of a Chihuahua: a stout body, a short, pointed muzzle, large round dark eyes, and big ears that stand erect on his apple-shaped head. Like the majority of dogs of his breed, Riley is chestnut in color.

Riley began his life in a Missouri puppy mill. Relegated to a small crate, neglected and abused, he had a tough start in life. Once it was determined that he was not suitable for breeding, he was left to die, receiving little food or water. Fortunately for Riley, the police came calling. The owner was arrested, and the animals of various breeds were turned over to a rescue organization.

Many miles north, in Michigan, Barb and Mike were in the process of looking specifically for a Chihuahua puppy. When Mike inquired at a pet supply store, he learned that a rescue group would be bringing a number of dogs to a local vet for adoption on the following Saturday. Among them was one Chihuahua.

Something that would make me remember what joy felt like. Something miraculous, something magical, something I couldn't believe existed. Something like . . . a chihuahua?
Mary Beth Crain

As soon as they arrived at the location, Mike and Barb saw the little dog being cradled in the arms of a young girl. Oh, those soulful eyes, those adorable ears. The little girl, whose mother was helping with the adoptions, handed the little guy over to Mike. First their eyes connected, and then the tiny animal situated himself in Mike's cradled arm. From that moment on, it was a done deal. Mike and Barb named him Riley because they intended to see that he lived the "life of Riley." And sure enough, with their children grown, the Chihuahua received more love and attention than he could have dreamed of, if in fact dogs dream of such things.

Soon enough, though, Mike and Barb realized that Riley had a number of fears. The sound of thunder would send him rushing for the head of the bed, where he would cower there on the pillow, his little body trembling violently. The sound of the garbage truck sent him running for cover. Though he seemed happy and affectionate with Mike and Barb, visitors terrified him. He would run for the bedroom or scoot under the sofa or a chair each time the doorbell rang. Since Chihuahuas are known to be courageous and bold by nature, Riley's humans concluded that his uncharacteristic fearfulness was the result of his time in the puppy mill.

> *You answered my*
> *prayer and came when*
> *I was in need. You told*
> *me, "Don't worry!"*
> *You rescued me and*
> *saved my life.*
> Lamentations 3:56–58
> CEV

For three years now, Mike and Barb have been working to renew Riley's fragile psyche, and it's working. Their steady love and encouragement are helping him become the dog God created him to be.

Many times we humans let our fears control us, as well—fear of standing out in the crowd, fear of failure, fear of confrontation, fear of change, fear of the unknown, fear of death;

and there are so many others. Some have even allowed these fears to take over their lives. When this happens, the only way

The LORD is my light and my salvation — whom shall I fear? The LORD is the stronghold of my life — of whom shall I be afraid? Psalm 27:1 NIV

out is to reprogram our minds. Riley has Mike and Barb to help him, but we have a helper, too. God is saying, "Trust me. Give me your fears. Let me help you replace your fearful thoughts with joy and peace."

Sometimes we may feel that our fears are too big to overcome. It could be that we have suffered at the hands of others, just as Riley did. Our minds may be flooded with images of abuse or terror or neglect that send us running for cover and trembling uncontrollably. Even these fears are no match for God's patient love and compassion. Life was meant to be lived and enjoyed. We need to refuse to let fear and trembling rob us of this precious gift.

Lend Me Your Ear

The purpose of life is not to be happy —
but to matter, to be productive, to be
useful, to have it make some difference
that you have lived at all.

Leo Rosten

Sometimes we get to thinking that we are "no good to nobody." We reason that we aren't talented enough, financially stable enough, or smart enough to make any significant contribution to the lives of others. But God has given each one of us the ability to do just that. Who would have thought a pound dog named Sasha would be able to provide any kind of needed service to those around her, but she did. She found her God-given gift, and you can, too.

The Canadian-based organization that brought Sasha into Ken's life offered only a small amount of information about her. She was rescued from an animal shelter, as are most of the dogs they train to assist the hearing-impaired. Ken isn't greatly concerned about her origins; he's just happy to have her in his life. Sasha, a small black Poodle/Schnauzer mix, or schnoodle, seems just as happy to be with Ken.

Ken has been losing his hearing gradually for the past ten years from a condition called otosclerosis. This condition reduces the ability of the three tiny bones in the middle ear to move efficiently. With his hearing becoming progressively worse, Ken suffered another blow when his wife, Margie, died. Grief-stricken and facing the probable loss of his independence, Ken slipped into depression. It was then that his daughter took him to see the doctor who told him about a resource he had never imagined existed—hearing ear dogs.

Of all the animals, surely the dog is the only one that really shares our life, helps in our work, and has a place in our recreation.
Fernand Mery

With the help of his daughter, his medical doctor, and his hearing specialist, Ken collected the records needed and completed the lengthy application. Once qualified, Ken spent twelve days at the training center working with Sasha and gaining personal, hands-on experience in handling and caring for her.

Like most hearing ear dogs, Sasha is high energy, is highly motivated, and loves to work. The two-year-old has been trained to alert Ken to a number of sounds around the household, such as the smoke alarm, telephone, doorbell (even someone knocking on the door), oven timer, alarm clock, and someone calling his name. Once she has alerted Ken, she escorts him to the origin of the sound. Sasha rarely leaves Ken's side. She knows her job, and she does it faithfully and confidently.

Sasha's closeness has also helped Ken emerge from his depression and start to live his life again. She gets excited when the grandchildren come to visit, but even then, she remains vigilant to her duties. Sasha also makes it possible for Ken to get out of the house. Her bright yellow leash signifies that she has been trained as a hearing ear dog and is welcome in public places of all kinds.

Let the favor of the Lord our God be upon us, and prosper for us the work of our hands — O prosper the work of our hands!
Psalm 90:17 NRSV

By any standard, Sasha is an amazing animal. In addition to her technical skills, she greatly decreases Ken's sense of loneliness and isolation. Her constant companionship is helping him deal with his grieving heart and stay tuned in to life.

Anyone can see that this was a match made in heaven. A lost and abandoned pound dog with a dim future found something to live for, and a lonely widower with a disability found a cheerful, friendly companion, a respite from grief and depression, and a way to continue living on his own in the house he and Margie shared for most of their married life.

At some point almost all of us question our purpose in life. We wonder how we can make a difference, and too often we shake our heads and decide that we don't have anything to offer or we are too limited by our circumstances. We do nothing, and in the process, we miss the blessings that come from being useful and making a difference in the world.

We are what he has made us, created in Christ Jesus for good works, which God prepared beforehand to be our way of life.
Ephesians 2:10 NRSV

Bright, energetic little Sasha must have wondered what difference she could make sitting there on the cold concrete floor of her cage at the animal shelter. But God had a plan for her. He sent someone who recognized her potential and helped her become what she was created to be.

God has a plan for our lives, as well. When we reach out to him, he will help us identify our potential. It might be something we've always known or something we've never considered. With God's help and hard work, we can make a difference, just as Sasha is doing.

Learning to Trust—Again!

Enjoy GOD, cheer when you see him! Father of orphans, champion of widows, is God in his holy house. God makes homes for the homeless, leads prisoners to freedom.

Psalm 68:4–6 MSG

Trust is a natural response. Newborn babies trust that someone will see that they are kept warm, fed, and cradled. They expect it. Distrust, on the other hand, is learned. When we are subjected to hurt, abuse, or neglect, trust crumbles. From there, we become more and more distrusting unless someone comes along who can teach us to trust again. Dogs, too, deserve a chance to trust again.

Greyhounds are the fastest dogs in the world, capable of reaching speeds of more than forty miles per hour. For centuries, they were used to chase down deer and wild boar. But since the early years of the twentieth century, they have been used primarily as racers. At its pinnacle of popularity in the late 1980s, tens of thousands of greyhounds were bred for the sole purpose of supplying North America's sixty dog tracks. And once their racing days were over, these precious animals were unceremoniously disposed of.

Alice, a tan and white female, was born on a puppy farm, where she was kept in a crate. At one year of age, she was moved to a kennel and began her racing career. During that time, she knew nothing of the world except her crate, the starting box, and the little mechanical rabbit on the inside rail of the racetrack. By the age of three, her career was over. Not so long ago, that would have meant certain death, but the decline in the racing industry and reforms in its governance have made a difference. Alice was turned over to a greyhound adoption agency.

> *He is your friend, your partner, your defender, your dog. . . . He will be yours, faithful and true, to the last beat of his heart. You owe it to him to be worthy of such devotion.*
> Trudy Truman

The beautiful, sleek athlete was justifiably terrified at first. After all, she had never ridden in a car, been inside a house, or seen a child or even another breed of dog. She had never slept outside her crate or experienced anything other than her working world. Alice was not accustomed to affection or human kindness, just the clinical gloved hands of those whose job it was to lead her into the starting box and then back into her crate.

As soon as she arrived at the adoption center, Alice was bathed and dipped, and given a new collar and ID tag. Then Alice became Sassy—a new name to begin a new life. Once her medical workup was complete, she was turned over to the volunteers who would do their best to restore her trust. They gently stroked her and spoke to her in a reassuring tone. And they put her on a strict feeding schedule so she would begin to trust that she would not go hungry. Slowly they helped her acclimate to the real world.

In their care, Sassy began to relax, and the innate characteristics of her breed began to surface. Larry and Joel, two of the volunteers, spent a lot of time with Sassy. They were determined to get to know her and draw her out of her shell. As her defenses came down, they tested her compatibility with children, strangers, and other animals. Sassy passed with overwhelming success.

> *May the God of hope fill you with all joy and peace in believing, so that you may abound in hope by the power of the Holy Spirit.*
> Romans 15:13 NRSV

Finally the day came for Sassy to meet her new family. The Clarksons had also been preparing at home and impressing upon their children that Sassy would need to be treated kindly and thoughtfully. It would be an almost overpowering situation for Sassy. She would have to leave the volunteers she had grown used to for a family of strangers. But when Carl, Maggie, seven-year-old Kendra, and four-year-old Logan encountered Sassy for the first time in the waiting room of the center, Sassy went right to them, responding warmly to their outstretched hands.

We're never so vulnerable than when we trust someone—but paradoxically, if we cannot trust, neither can we find love or joy.
Walter Anderson

Sassy has been with the Clarksons for three years now. They say she is a sweet animal, playful, and a bit lazy. And why shouldn't she be? they reason. She's had her career, and now she should enjoy the privileges of retirement.

If some of us, like Sassy, have never experienced the comfort of human love, God has volunteered to gently teach us to trust again. He will help us replace our less-than-good experiences with his constant love and tender care. And once we have learned to reach out and trust again, he will send loving people into our lives, just as he did with Sassy.

Death to the Cobra

You will tread upon the lion and the cobra; you will trample the great lion and the serpent. "Because he loves me," says the LORD, "I will rescue him; I will protect him."

Psalm 91:13–14 NIV

Society in general tends to be clannish. In ordinary times, most of us tend to seek out those who look and act as we do, those who share our opinions and world-views. But in times of extraordinary danger, walls that once separated us come down. We become simply human beings brought together in a dance of self-preservation. A dog named Leo and a cat named Bosky can attest that it must be the same for animals.

Sudha Khristmukti laughs at those who say dogs and cats can't get along. Her black mutt dog, Leo, and her sassy brown alley cat, Bosky, share the same plate and any choice bones she gives them. These two have dismissed the natural enmity between dogs and cats and allied themselves for one purpose—to protect Sudha and the compound in which they live.

In the small town of Gujarat, India, where Sudha lives, there is no such thing as animal or pest control. It isn't unusual for deadly cobras, vipers, and kraits to wander through neighborhoods located near swamps and vacant fields. Once, Sudha saw a cobra sitting on the compound wall swallowing a squirrel whole. On another occasion, she saw one crawl from behind a drum of water. With summer temperatures near 110 degrees, she surmised that the predator was drawn by the shade and the cool, wet ground.

> *The one absolutely unselfish friend that man can have in this selfish world, the one that never deserts him, the one that never proves ungrateful or treacherous, is his dog.*
> George G. Vest

Those bitten by these poisonous snakes have little chance of survival. Extremely potent, cobra venom affects the central nervous system, producing cardiac and respiratory failure within two to six hours. Few survive, since antivenin is not available in Gujarat. Even the hospitals don't stock it. Victims must be taken five hundred miles away to Mumbai. Most are either dead on arrival or too far gone to save.

Considering these facts, it's no wonder Sudha was terrified when she was awakened from a deep sleep by a bloodcurdling hiss inside the compound. She crept far enough out her door on that hot, sultry night to see that Leo and Bosky had cornered a large cobra under a bougainvillea tree.

As the two barked and meowed, Sudha shook off her grogginess and went into offensive mode. If humans were no match for a cobra, she knew her beloved pets were staring into the face of death. She began to pray as she reached for her air gun, a gift from a missionary friend.

Since her gun fired a single pellet, she would have to keep her eyes on the snake while reloading after each shot. In addition, the gun didn't have much range. She would have to get within six to ten feet for the pellets to have a significant impact. This was Sudha's only weapon, useful for killing house lizards, bats, or squirrels, but not particularly effective with cobras. She knew it would take fifteen to twenty shots directly into the fanning hood to bring down the beast.

> I appeal to you, brothers and sisters, by the name of our Lord Jesus Christ, that all of you should be in agreement and that there be no divisions among you, but that you be united in the same mind and the same purpose.
> 1 Corinthians 1:10
> NRSV

Heart pounding, Sudha turned on the porch lights and got her first real look at the large jet-black creature with a white underbelly. Leo and Bosky were doggedly holding the monster at bay while dodging its venomous strikes. Sudha knew she could not afford to miss.

With her first shot in the chamber, she edged around to find the best angle—and fired. A loud hiss told her she had struck the cobra. She quickly took a pellet from her pajama pocket, reloaded, and fired again. By the time she had fired eighteen pellets, she was bathed in perspiration and trembling uncontrollably. But inspired by her faithful pets, she could not let the snake slither away.

We cannot be separated in interest or divided in purpose. We stand together until the end.
Woodrow Wilson

Quickly reloading, she shot once again into the cobra's hood, and this time it could hold its head up no longer. Seeing his opportunity, Leo fearlessly pounced on the back of the cobra's head and finished it off.

Sudha, Leo, and Bosky stood watching the cobra until it stopped writhing. Then, happy to be alive, the three congratulated one another. Working together, they had successfully defended themselves against a thick, jet-black eight-foot killer.

In times of danger, we rarely have an opportunity to choose our battle mates. We simply stand together for expediency's sake. If we are able to put our differences aside to defend ourselves, maybe we should consider laying them aside altogether.

Sheena the Great!

True heroism is remarkably sober, very undramatic. It is not the urge to surpass all others at whatever cost, but the urge to serve others at whatever cost.
Arthur Ashe

The heart of a hero often abides unseen until an extreme circumstance draws it to the surface and thrusts it into action. At those times, unlikely champions rise to the challenge and show their true mettle, proving that heroism is more about spirit and inner resolve than big talk and brawn. Real heroes don't always come dressed for the part. That's true of our canine friends, as well.

In Gujarat, India, where Sudha Khristmukti lives, there are no animal rescue groups or shelters. Only one veterinarian serves the area, and he is occupied full-time with the buffalo, cows, goats, sheep, and camels belonging to the local farmers.

Stray dogs wander about the neighborhoods in pitiable conditions. With no garbage collection system, the poor animals forage for scraps of rotten food discarded in the streets.

Often badly malnourished and attacked by roaming dog gangs, it isn't unusual for some to be missing a foreleg or hind leg. Many are struck by cars or buses on the highway or are harassed by local children who throw rocks at them. Female strays have an even bleaker existence. Most are forced to deliver litter after litter with no hope of seeing their offspring to adulthood.

A few months after Leo, Sudha's amazing dog, died quietly at the age of seventeen years, another special animal came into her life. Sudha's mother, who was a physician, did her best to care for the human needs around her but also had much compassion for the birds and cats she encountered—and especially the often-injured and terribly neglected stray dogs. One day she rescued a litter of newborn puppies. Despite her efforts, just one survived. She wrapped the scrawny female in a blanket and presented it to Sudha. At least they could save that one from the indignities of the street. Sudha and her mother named the pup Sheena.

> *A really companionable and indispensable dog is an accident of nature. You can't get it by breeding for it, and you can't buy it with money. It just happens along.*
>
> E. B. White

After a warm bath and a flurry of flea powder, Sheena drank a huge bowl of milk and curled up in Sudha's lap for a long nap. A few weeks later she was ready to be out in the compound where she rolled in the grass, watched birds with great fascination (especially the crows), and chased squirrels. At two months, she chewed up every pair of Sudha's footwear. Chew bones intended to dissuade her were ignored. Sheena and a tortoise in the yard often went nose-to-nose.

Sheena was a light shade of brown with brown eyes and a black mouth. Not much more than thirty-five pounds full-grown, she would not have been tagged as a guard dog. But there was more to the little female stray than met the eye. When it came to protecting the compound, she took on all comers. She had no tolerance for squirrels and chased away or killed chameleons and lizards. She took on field mice and large rats that tried to creep into the fenced area. Once she killed a three-pound rat and a rat snake both in one night.

> *You light a lamp for me. The LORD, my God, lights up my darkness. In your strength I can crush an army; with my God I can scale any wall.*
> Psalm 18:28–29 NLT

Then one sweltering tropical evening, she begged to be let outside where it was cooler. It was there that, like Leo her predecessor, she went up against a seven-foot cobra and won. Sudha and her mother watched from the bedroom window as Sheena stalked the snake and carried out a precision strike to the back of the cobra's head. After assuring herself that the beast was dead, she picked it up in her teeth and flung it against the compound wall.

No one would have fancied the diminutive female—who barely survived her own birth—a hero, but that's exactly what she was.

The LORD does not look at the things man looks at. Man looks at the outward appearance, but the LORD looks at the heart.
1 Samuel 16:7 NIV

Underneath that unassuming exterior, she had the passion and drive of a warrior.

Too often we overlook the true heroes in our midst—the single parent, the persevering teacher, the stalwart employee, the dedicated volunteer. There are so many who quietly and unassumingly rise up to defend our corporate well-being, confronting injustice and evil wherever they find it. Their passion comes from their hearts, and their great and often unsung deeds benefit us all. We owe each one of them our appreciation.

Hard Times, Soft Heart

Suffering becomes beautiful when anyone bears great calamities with cheerfulness, not through insensibility but through greatness of mind.
Aristotle

Some people suffer greatly and as a result become hardened and angry, locked in a perpetual state of warfare with everyone and everything around them. Still others embrace the suffering, allowing it to make them more compassionate, forgiving, and appreciative of simple pleasures. Everyone faces some type of suffering at some point in life, and each person must choose how he or she will respond. One sweet dog is an example of what it means to accept your suffering.

Merri Grace is part chocolate Labrador and part blue heeler. She has a good life with loving, responsible owners and the companionship of two dogs whose stories have already been told—Chewie and Miss Pip. But the first chapter of her life was difficult and painful.

Merri was purchased in the parking lot of a department store.

She was intended to be a Christmas present for the children of a single mother. But no one expected the cute little puppy to grow so quickly and overwhelm the tiny apartment where the family lived or place even more strain on their fragile finances. Whether Merri was simply put outside or decided to leave on her own is not known. She wandered around the apartment complex for a few days until another resident, a woman named Reisa, knocked on the original owner's door and inquired about her. The single mom passed along the vital information to her neighbor—how she came to have the dog, the dog's name (Merri Grace), and her age (six months)—but confessed that there was no way she could keep her any longer.

> *Labradors are lousy watchdogs. They usually bark when there is a stranger about, but it is an expression of unmitigated joy at the chance to meet somebody new, not a warning.*
> Norman Strung

Reisa took Merri Grace in for a few nights, but she was already over the limit of animals allowed by the apartment complex. She looked long and hard for someone to take Merri permanently. A few days later, a man from a neighboring subdivision called in response to a flyer Reisa had posted at a nearby park. The man came to see Merri and noted what a sweet and friendly animal she was. He took her home, and Reisa thought Merri's story had ended happily. But little more than a month later, Merri reappeared in the courtyard of the apartment complex. Though her sweet nature was still intact, Reisa noticed she had lost weight and appeared to have been beaten across her back. A few days later, Reisa witnessed an encounter between Merri and a car. The driver grazed her side as he did his best to miss her. Merri walked away from the incident with a limp. Later that day, Reisa saw neighborhood boys throwing rocks at the poor dog. It looked like Merri had run out of options.

> *After you have suffered for a little while, the God of all grace, who has called you to his eternal glory in Christ, will himself restore, support, strengthen, and establish you.*
> 1 Peter 5:10 NRSV

For the second time, Reisa took Merri into her apartment. She treated her wounds as best she could and provided her with fresh food and water. As Merri began to improve, Reisa looked in earnest for someone who would love and care for this resilient dog.

Reisa's strategy was to take Merri along with her on errands as often as possible with the hope someone would be drawn to her simple beauty and personal charm. One day as Reisa was dropping off her husband's golf shoes at the golf course where he worked, she saw David, her husband's co-worker. The magic happened. David liked the way Merri stood straight and looked him in the eye. He admired her gentle disposition and friendly demeanor. When David found out she was available, he agreed to take her home.

Today Merri Grace is happy and well-adjusted. Despite her physical and emotional scars, she seems to bear no malice toward anyone. In fact, people and dogs alike seem to be drawn by her humble, gentle, and loving nature. She is the picture of doggy contentment and grace.

> *We also rejoice in our sufferings, because we know that suffering produces perseverance; perseverance, character; and character, hope.*
> **Romans 5:3–4** NIV

We would all like to think we can escape suffering in our lives, but there really are no exceptions. When we encounter painful situations, we have a decision to make. Will we let our suffering bury us in anger and self-pity or will we take our lead from Merri Grace and refuse to let our suffering defeat us? In this way we disburse the suffering, destroying its power over us and opening us up to a better future.

The Best of Intentions

Fortunate those whose crimes are carted off, whose sins are wiped clean from the slate. Fortunate the person against whom the Lord does not keep score.

Romans 4:7–8 MSG

Most of us have on occasion set out with conviction and passion to do something good, something we thought we were supposed to do, only to find that we ended up doing more harm than good. This very thing happened to a dog named Samson, whose passion to guard and protect caused him to accidentally injure one of the humans he loved most in the world.

When Alice and Benny moved their family to a thirty-acre spread, they immediately realized they needed a reliable guard dog to patrol the property and ward off intruders. They found what they were looking for when a friend gave them a beautiful black Labrador puppy. They named him Samson, Sammy for short.

Sammy grew quickly, and as he did, his family began to notice a collar of rough hair just below his head that identified him not as the purebred they had thought him to be but a Lab/Chow mix. This, they reasoned, would only make him better at his job. Chows, after all, are known to be fiercely protective.

In fact, Sammy did turn out to be a wonderful dog by any standard. Solid black and more than ninety pounds, he definitely served as a deterrent as he lay on the porch or walked quietly around the yard.

Everyone says they have the perfect dog. Come on, folks. What you mean is you have a dog whose crimes you are willing to overlook for the sake of love.
Helga Carver

The family, however, considered him harmless. He was affectionate and gentle with the children, often demonstrating his devotion to them by laying his head in their laps and nuzzling their hands. Alice describes him as confident, steady, and unruffled by circumstances. Perhaps that is why they were so surprised by the incident that occurred at the front of their property one overcast spring day.

Alice and Benny's oldest daughter, Rachel, had decided to take Sammy for a walk up the driveway and around the yard. Sammy was happy to go along. It should have been a happy together time for the two of them, but near the end of the driveway, Sammy spotted another dog. When the dog walked toward them in an aggressive manner, the guard dog, the protector, and perhaps the fierce Chow that occupied some part of Sammy's canine psyche, suddenly came to the surface. He ran at the other dog, and they were quickly embroiled in a fight.

Rachel had never seen Sammy act in this way, and she was terrified. She called his name repeatedly, trying to get him to stop fighting, but he was committed and paid no attention to her. Finally, Rachel decided she had to intervene and tried to physically pull Sammy away from the other dog. Having placed herself in harm's way, she was bitten on the arm and pushed to the ground, not by the unknown dog but by her own precious Sammy.

> *Learn to be patient,*
> *so that you will please*
> *God and be given what*
> *he has promised.*
> Hebrews 10:36 CEV

Benny heard Rachel's cries and came running. He separated the dogs and carried Rachel to the house. Though Rachel's injuries were not serious, Sammy refused to leave her side. Rachel patted his head repeatedly and tried to reassure him. "Don't be sad, Sammy," she would say. "I know you never meant for me to get hurt."

At one time or another, most of us have experienced the angst Sammy must have felt that day. We set out to do the right thing, the thing that is expected of us, and yet somehow it goes wrong and we end up hurting someone we love. We try to comfort a friend and say the wrong thing. We try to help a loved one and end up making matters worse. Our good intentions sometimes go awry—no doubt about it. So what are we supposed to do next?

Sammy seemed to worry over Rachel's injuries. But after a time, the guard dog let himself off the hook. He went back to keeping a steely eye on the property and would have undoubtedly defended it again just as fiercely as he had the first time.

> *Victorious living does not mean perfect living in the sense of living without flaw, but it does mean adequate living, and that can be consistent with many mistakes.*
> E. Stanley Jones

We should follow Sammy's example. When things go wrong, we must not let it keep us from doing our best to help and protect those we love. We shouldn't back away from conflict or lose confidence in ourselves. Instead, we need to make our apologies and get back to the business of living.

Our culture makes severe demands on the dog. We humans accept mostly on hearsay, the premise that "dog is man's best friend" and let it go at that. For the dog, this is a debatable issue. He knows that, if anything, the reverse holds true. It is man who is dog's best friend.

Stephen Baker

Love Without Limitations

Love has nothing to do with what you are expecting to get—only with what you are expecting to give—which is everything.
Katharine Hepburn

One of the most common words in the English language is *love*. We apply it to everything from baseball to relationships. We should be quite good at it. But our furry friends far surpass us when it comes to loving unconditionally. Our love is often anchored to expectations, achievements, and actions. Maybe we can learn a few things from a feisty dog named Bonnie.

In time, Alice and Benny realized they needed more than one dog to guard their thirty-acre property. As they discussed the type of dog they might be looking for, Alice suggested a white dog. During the day, the big black Labrador Sammy could easily be seen, but at night he was virtually invisible. A white dog would help to discourage intruders after dark.

Some friends had rescued a Louisiana Catahoula mix from the pound. They loved the dog dearly, but she soon grew too large for their small yard. Bonnie was a year and a half when she joined Sammy on border patrol.

Though she was not a purebred, Bonnie looked like a Louisiana Catahoula, or leopard dog. Her short coat of coarse hair was mostly white with black confetti specks. With a broad chest and long body and weighing in at almost ninety pounds, she looked the part of a true guardian. In addition, her breed is known to be independent, protective, and territorial—perfect for the job at hand.

I think dogs are the most amazing creatures; they give unconditional love. For me, they are the role model for being alive.
Gilda Radner

Alice and Benny noticed right away that Bonnie was extremely bright. Her yapping and body language sounded and looked like she was trying to carry on a conversation with them. And when asked the whereabouts of Sammy or one of the children, she would quite deliberately point them in the right direction with her head.

Bonnie was unusually affectionate and loving as well. She always greeted Alice by batting her eyes and rubbing her head against Alice's leg. She demonstrated her love for Benny and the children in similar ways.

One evening the family noticed that Bonnie was not around at nightfall. Though they called for her, she did not appear. When she hadn't returned by the next afternoon, it was time to go looking. Alice and Benny jumped in their pickup and drove out to the fence line. From there they crawled over the fence and called for her. Right away they could hear her raspy bark.

A few hundred feet ahead, they found Bonnie with her paw caught in a trap. Sadly, they realized she could well have been there for thirty hours. Benny approached her slowly, knowing that injured dogs are prone to aggressive behavior. But he needn't have worried. As he released her foot, she ran around in circles on her three good legs, yapping and rubbing her body up against their legs and expressing how glad she was to see them. Even while her paw was healing, Bonnie never showed the slightest anger toward her human family for the accident that had befallen her. Hurt or unhurt, she loved them.

> *This is my commandment, that you love one another as I have loved you. No one has greater love than this, to lay down one's life for one's friends.*
> John 15:12–13 NRSV

Many dogs, like Bonnie, have a tremendous capacity for unconditional love. They don't assign blame, and they are quick to forgive and forget. They are free of judgment and do not assess their masters based on education, looks, intelligence, or even character. They simply love them without qualification.

For human beings, loving unconditionally is somewhat more complicated. Or is it? Loving unconditionally does not mean we must condone certain actions or allow others to use and abuse us. In fact, unconditional love calls on us to lovingly speak the truth and require certain standards of respectability and responsibility.

"Though the mountains be shaken and the hills be removed, yet my unfailing love for you will not be shaken nor my covenant of peace be removed," says the LORD, who has compassion on you.
Isaiah 54:10 NIV

The essence of unconditional love is strength and resilience. It will not shatter in the hard times. It says, "I'm not going anywhere. I will be here today, tomorrow, and the day after that. I love you for who you are on the inside, despite your flaws. My love does not demand that you do things my way or say what I want to hear." Unconditional love does not come easily to humans. It stretches us, especially when we feel hurt and helpless. But that's when we need to follow Bonnie's example.

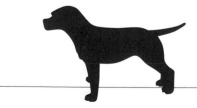

Hey, Jordy, It's for You!

The good news is that you really don't know how great you can be, how much you can love, what you can accomplish, and what your potential is!

Anne Frank

Some people never even try to reach their potential. Some achieve only what others convince them they are capable of. But some people aren't satisfied with the expectations of others. They aim for the stars and refuse to believe there is anything they can't do if they set their minds to it. Some dogs are like that, too. They are certain they can rise far above their doggyness.

Jordy is a full-grown golden retriever who lives with his people, Dale and Charlene, in an Iowa farming community. He belonged originally to an elderly neighbor who was moving away and had to give him up. She described him as a smart, energetic dog who had been a great help to her. Then she added, "Jordy is the cleverest animal I've ever seen. I honestly believe he thinks he's a human."

Even with that enthusiastic endorsement, Jordy surprised his new owners. His personal initiative was astonishing. Charlene would wonder aloud where she left her shoes and, just like that, Jordy would appear with one of them in his mouth. After depositing it at her feet, he would race off to get the other. Soon they were simply saying, "Jordy, go get this" or "Go get that," and sure enough, he would find what they were asking for and deliver it to them. If something was too big for him to carry in his teeth, he would lock on and drag it.

> *A member poll found that 33 percent of dog owners admit to talking to their dogs on the phone and leaving messages for them on their answering machines.*
> American Animal Hospital Association

During the time with his previous owner, Jordy apparently learned how to turn knobs and open doors. With a little encouragement, Charlene taught him to close them behind him. Jordy could wind and unwind the garden hose, herd the chickens into the coop, and even help Dale clean up the yard by picking up sticks and pieces of litter. Jordy was also an excellent watchdog, sending up an alarm when any unknown person or vehicle came up the long driveway.

This remarkable golden retriever has even learned how to get the porch glider moving before he jumps on. Dale and Charlene are impressed with their adopted farm dog. They brag about him to their friends and love giving demonstrations. Jordy is quite the crowd pleaser. There is one trick, however, that they agree is his most amazing. Jordy likes to talk on the phone.

The first time it happened, it was intended to be a joke. Dale was away from the house and called home to ask Charlene a question. As usual, Jordy parked himself in front of Charlene and sat there as if awaiting his turn. So on a whim, Charlene told Dale, "Hang on, I think Jordy wants to say something!" With that, she held out the phone to Jordy. The dog stared at Charlene and then at the phone, turning his head from side to side. But when he heard Dale's voice, he went wild, jumping and barking and carrying on. When Dale said, "Jordy, go get my boots," the dog gave one more confident *arf* and bolted for the mudroom. The task finished, Jordy parked himself again at Charlene's feet and quietly waited for another chance to talk to Dale.

Such confidence as this is ours through Christ before God. Not that we are competent in ourselves to claim anything for ourselves, but our competence comes from God.
2 Corinthians 3:4–5
NIV

The phone conversations are now routine when either Dale or Charlene is away from home. Dale says there is only one problem. Jordy comes running whenever the phone rings, thinking every call is for him.

Many times, we allow other people to define our potential, and once we take someone else's word that we can't do something, we usually can't. High achievers, like Jordy, seem to ignore such punitive limitations. It may have taken one hundred tries before Jordy was able to turn the knob and open the door, but he succeeded because he believed he could do it and wouldn't give up until he made it work.

I forget what is behind, and I struggle for what is ahead. I run toward the goal, so that I can win the prize of being called to heaven.
Philippians 3:13–14
CEV

Just as Jordy exceeded expectations and learned to open doors and talk on the phone, so, too, can we go beyond our self-imposed limitations. We can believe in our boundless potential and shoot for the stars. If our hearts urge us to try something, we should go for it. If we believe we can do it, we can.

We Call Her Jazzy

We cannot live for ourselves alone. Our lives are connected by a thousand invisible threads, and along these sympathetic fibers, our actions run as causes and return to us as results.

Herman Melville

We often miss out on the blessing of helping others because we imagine to do so would require time, money, or physical effort we don't have. The task just seems so big and impossible. And yet a little time can help in a big way; acts of human kindness are typically free, and the physical effort required may be minimal. Sometimes all you need is a handful of ebony fluff.

Carol calls them her special people. For a number of years now, she has spent every Wednesday afternoon holding a sing-along with the residents of the elder-care facility near her home. She knows every resident by name and takes great joy in hearing them sing out enthusiastically. Some can no longer remember the details of their lives, yet they can recall most of the words to the familiar songs and hymns she plays. That's the power of music.

Each week, Carol arrives midafternoon and greets each person before heading to the grand piano that occupies one corner of the sunny community room. As she begins to play, the residents join in and the room fills with singing. Carol enjoys this time immensely. It's her way of reaching out to others.

Carol first visited the facility with her church group, and she was touched by the loneliness, boredom, and unhappiness on the faces of the frail residents. So many of those wonderful folks, she later learned, had few visitors, no one to listen to them, no one to laugh with them, and no one to hug them. She vowed to make a difference and to bring some sunshine into their lives. She could see that the sing-alongs were helping, but her elderly friends needed more than she could give them.

If a dog jumps into your lap, it is because he is fond of you, but if a cat does the same thing, it is because your lap is warmer.
Alfred North Whitehead

Carol isn't sure where the idea came from. Maybe God whispered in her ear. All she can say is that it popped into her head one day as she was praying, and she wondered why she hadn't thought of it sooner.

The following Wednesday, Carol entered the community room just as she had so many times before, with one tiny difference. As she greeted each resident, she held out a tiny black puppy, no more than a handful of fluff. "My name is Carol," she said for the sake of the new faces and the regulars with failed memories, "and this is the newest member of my family. She's only six weeks old, and her name is Jazzy. She's a toy Poodle of the teacup variety," Carol told them. "Isn't she wonderful?"

Carol took one man's withered hands and cupped them. Then she placed the little pup into them. A hush fell over the room as everyone focused on the old man and little Jazzy. The man never took his eyes off her. Then his face lit up, and he said, "I had me a dog once." Soon everyone was sharing about the dogs they once had and taking turns passing little Jazzy from one person to the next. It was some time before the singing began that Wednesday, but no one minded.

Serve wholeheartedly, as if you were serving the Lord, not men, because you know that the Lord will reward everyone for whatever good he does.
Ephesians 6:7–8 NIV

Little Jazzy has been a fixture at the elder-care facility ever since. She comes with Carol every week and hops from lap to lap, relishing the little treats her admirers save for her from their lunches. During the sing-alongs, she positions her body on whatever lap looks inviting and settles back to ensure the maximum amount of petting. She's happy when she's with Carol's elderly friends—and the feeling is mutual.

Carol wouldn't think of going to sing-alongs without Jazzy. She tells her friends that to do so could mean she'd be booed and pelted by back pillows and tissue boxes. She isn't about to take that kind of risk, she tells them with a laugh.

We often forget the simple joy animals bring to life. Big or small, they leave us feeling that we've made a life-giving connection with a creature that sees us and accepts us as we really are.

> *Each of you has been blessed with one of God's many wonderful gifts to be used in the service of others. So use your gift well.*
> 1 Peter 4:10 CEV

Our dogs may be too big to fit in someone's outstretched hands, but we can still find appropriate opportunities for our pets to bless the special people in our lives. Dogs have a remarkable rapport with hurting human beings. They are able to relate in situations where the most caring people cannot. They do what dogs do best—make us feel whole again.

Let Me Be Your Eyes

In helping others, we shall help ourselves,
for whatever good we give out completes
the circle and comes back to us.
Flora Edwards

The great hymn writer William Cowper wrote: "God moves in a mysterious way, his wonders to perform." It's true. His ways of doing things are often multifaceted. For example, in helping others, we often help ourselves. Stepping past fears and perceived limitations in order to help others actually strengthens and steadies us, and gives us a greater sense of purpose and direction. That's what happened when Daisy, a Shih Tzu, inspired a lonely woman to put her little dog's needs first.

Helen Sherman had always been a busy woman. She raised four children (three girls and one boy), looked after her husband, an accountant at a small local firm, taught third grade for thirty years at a nearby elementary school, and on Sundays and Wednesdays played the piano at Carbondale Community Church. But as the years went by, things changed for Helen. Her three girls married and moved away, and her husband, Roy, died unexpectedly at the age of sixty. Only her son, Guy, and his family remained in town.

At the age of sixty-three, Helen suffered another setback. She had to retire from teaching and give up playing piano because of an eye condition called macular degeneration. Though she was not technically blind, she had a blind spot in the center of each eye that made it impossible for her to drive, read music, or teach. As the condition worsened, Helen withdrew from activities until she was virtually homebound.

Dogs have the uncommon ability to bring out the best in their humans. No wonder God so often used them for his own purposes.
Trudy Truman

Helen's children heated up the phone lines trying to find a solution for their mother, but she dismissed all their ideas. Finally, Guy had an interesting thought that went something like this: *We could buy Mother a dog. Mother would have to walk the dog, which would require her to get out of the house and deal with life again.*

Helen's oldest daughter, Annie, did the research and passed it along to her siblings. Together they decided on a Shih Tzu (pronounced shē dzoo), a breed of active, alert toy dogs that originated in Tibet. They reasoned that a toy dog would be most appropriate for Helen because they are easier to handle and care for. And according to the literature, Shih Tzus are excellent companion dogs.

Through a newspaper ad, they were able to find a two-year-old named Daisy. She was a cutie, white with black ears, eyes, nose, and mouth. She was ten pounds of silky, wiggly wonderful. But when Guy and his wife, Jackie, presented Daisy to Helen, they once again encountered resistance.

"I don't want a dog," she protested. "How can I take care of a dog when I can barely take care of myself?"

As Jackie brought in and set up the dog paraphernalia, Guy tried to tell his mother about the breed and Daisy in particular, emphasizing the importance of walking her three times a day. But Helen was having none of it. Finally, there was nothing left to do but leave the dog and scram!

> *The LORD is my shepherd, I shall not want. He makes me lie down in green pastures; he leads me beside still waters; he restores my soul.*
> Psalm 23:1–3 NRSV

Once she and Helen were alone, Daisy did her own sell job. She followed Helen from room to room and snuggled up with her on the couch. That night when Helen climbed into bed, Daisy was right there with her, a soft ball of comfort for lonely, sleepless nights.

Helen quickly came to depend on Daisy, but she still had reservations about taking the sweet little animal for walks. In the beginning, she put Daisy out in the small backyard and encouraged her to run around. But Helen knew in her heart she was not doing enough. Eventually, her desire to give Daisy the exercise she needed overrode her fear of leaving the house. One day she snapped on Daisy's leash, took a deep breath, and put one foot in front of the other.

You have made known to me the path of life; you will fill me with joy in your presence, with eternal pleasures at your right hand.
Psalm 16:11 NIV

Early walks were confined to the sidewalk in front of the house, but eventually Helen gained the courage to venture to a nearby park. Once there, the little Shih Tzu served as the perfect conversation starter. Within a week, Daisy had ten new friends, and Helen had two. With Daisy's help, Helen learned there was still a place for her in the world.

Her love for Daisy and determination to meet Daisy's needs opened the door to a new life for Helen. It seems counterintuitive, even a little mysterious, but many of God's ways are.

Are You My Mother?

Few things in the world are more power-
ful than a positive push. A smile. A
word of optimism and hope. A "you
can do it" when things are tough.
Richard M. DeVos

Wouldn't it be great if all families were intact, loving, and supportive? But that just isn't the way it works in this crazy, mixed-up world. Fortunately, there are those who step up and fill the gap for those who are bereft, abandoned, and forgotten. These remarkable people and the people they mentor can sometimes be unlikely duos, but somehow they work; somehow they find a way to give what is needed.

Every once in a while on a slow news night, there will be a human-interest story about a baby chick who has been adopted by a Chihuahua somewhere in mainland China or an orphaned baby squirrel who is being cared for by a cocker spaniel in Seattle. One such story talked about a fawn that had been rejected by its mother and was being nurtured by two working dogs in a safari park.

This phenomenon is called imprinting. Apparently, it isn't uncommon for an abandoned or orphaned creature to form a strong attachment to another animal that is not its mother. This is particularly common with birds and ducks, which tend to imprint on the first moving thing they see. But it can certainly happen with bigger animals, as well.

Greg was a city kid. He grew up with four siblings in Kansas City. But every summer they visited their mother's younger brother's farm in south-

The one absolutely un-selfish friend that man can have in this selfish world, the one that never deserts him, the one that never proves ungrateful or treacherous is his dog.

George Graham Vest

eastern Indiana. Greg enjoyed their trips to see Uncle Gary. He loved animals, and there were always plenty around the place— dogs, cats, chickens, bunnies, squirrels, a few cows, and one pig. Greg's favorite was a gray and black German shepherd mix named Katie. For most of her life, she had been a hardworking farm dog, but as she grew older, she spent a lot of time resting on the porch or in the shade of a big elm behind Uncle Gary's house.

Katie was a gentle creature who never refused a good scratch from a human friend. She always got up to greet Greg when he came out of the house, aware that he usually had crackers or cookies in his pocket to share with her. He remembers using her soft body for a pillow while he spent lazy hours lying in the shade reading.

One summer the family went to the farm in early spring, right after school let out. After greeting Uncle Gary and helping carry their things inside, Greg went looking for Katie, who had failed to greet them in her usual way. He found her in the barn, surrounded by kittens. There were four in all, little bitty things. Katie didn't seem to care at all that they were crawling all over her.

Praise God, the Father of our Lord Jesus Christ! The Father is a merciful God, who always gives us comfort. He comforts us when we are in trouble, so that we can share that same comfort with others in trouble.
2 Corinthians 1:3–4
CEV

Later, Greg asked Uncle Gary about Katie and the kittens. "The mother died shortly after she gave birth," his uncle told him. "I fed them with an eyedropper until they were big enough to drink from a bowl. Then I made Katie their kitty-sitter. She's good with them, watches over those little orphans like they were a litter of her own pups."

Greg laughed when he saw Katie emerge from the barn with her brood right behind her, the kittens falling over one another to keep up with Katie. At night, snuggled into the warm barn straw, they slept as close to her as they could. Even after the kittens became full-grown cats, they were unabashedly affectionate with Katie. She was the only mother they had ever known.

Katie lived to be eleven years old. It was for her a happy and contented old age. Interestingly, subsequent litters of kittens followed their mothers to Katie's side. From surrogate mother she became surrogate grandmother and great-grandmother.

There is no shortage of orphans in our world. Many of them need the nurture of a loving parent. Someone who will lead them in the right direction and help them make a go of their lives. Someone who can look past the differences and realize that no matter who we are, we all face the same issues and need to learn the same lessons. Someone who is willing to be a parent for a child who has none. It might make for some unlikely duos. But Katie and her kitties prove that where there's a will, there's a way.

The Counselor, the Holy Spirit, whom the Father will send in my name, will teach you all things and will remind you of everything I have said to you.
John 14:26 NIV

Anything for a Laugh

Laughter sets the spirit free to move through even the most tragic circumstances. It helps us shake our heads clear, get our feet back under us, and restore our sense of balance and purpose.
Gerald Coffee

Health professionals tell us straight up that laughter is a powerful antidote for troubling circumstances, pain, and negative emotions. It is known to strengthen our immune systems, boost our energy, diminish pain, and protect us from the wear and tear of stress. Considering this, wouldn't it make sense to choose friends who make us laugh? And maybe we should choose our dogs that way, too!

Some people are just born funny. We all know the type. Remember the kid who spent an inordinate amount of time in the principal's office because he or she saw everything as material for stand-up comedy? Typically, there is a comic in every office, as well—someone who can find humor in the ludicrous, the annoying, and even the tragic. Taps, a Jack Russell terrier mix, has the capacity for humor, too.

Taps's people, John and Milly, say he never complains when they dress him up in little tap shoes, a doggy tuxedo, and a top hat. In fact, they swear he loves it. Milly says he's a comedian first and a showman second. If he falls over and gets a laugh, he'll hop back up and fall over repeatedly just to keep it coming.

John and Milly run a dance school in upstate New York. Since they spend so much time at the studio, they have always brought Taps along. They expected him to just hang out, content to watch the action, but the little dog had other ideas. John and Milly originally named him Garth—after Garth Brooks, their favorite country singer—but when they realized his aptitude for entertainment, they thought it prudent to give him a stage name: Sir Tapsalot, or Taps for short!

> *The great pleasure of a dog is that you make a fool of yourself with him and not only will he not scold you, he will make a fool of himself too.*
> Samuel Butler

In costume or out, Taps is a serious showman, determined to keep the students laughing. Before each session, Milly calls him in to get everyone excited and energized. Sometimes he just sits in front of the class, his white and tan body as still as a statue, staring straight ahead with his dark, almond-shaped eyes until someone starts giggling. Then he knows he has them where he wants them. He starts by wiggling his cute black nose and flipped-forward ears until the giggling reaches a fever pitch. That's when he launches into his full-out comedy routine, jumping in the air, running around in circles, walking on his back legs, falling over on his side. John says Taps will do just about anything for a laugh, and his antics never get old.

> *You have turned my mourning into joyful dancing. You have taken away my clothes of mourning and clothed me with joy, that I might sing praises to you and not be silent.*
> Psalm 30:11–12 NLT

Taps keeps John and Milly laughing at home, as well. John says Taps gets up on his back legs and dances in front of the TV when they are trying to watch the news, sticks his head as far into his water dish as he possibly can before popping it back out again, and does backflips off the furniture. He is a born clown.

For the past three years, Sir Tapsalot has been the opening act for the dance school's quarterly recitals. Because the recitals are in the evening, John and Milly feel for the parents who have already put in a long workday. Most of them are exhausted. Taps gets them laughing and in a mood to enjoy the show.

Wouldn't it be nice if we all had a Sir Tapsalot in our lives? We often live eyeball-to-eyeball with our troubles, internalizing all that worry and stress. And when we do, our bodies tighten up. We become exhausted and sore from the tension in our muscles, making us susceptible to depression and physical illness.

Laughter would seem to be God's gift for shaking off all that inner angst. After all, our troubles are always with us; they simply change their costumes. One year our troubles are medical, the next financial, and the next rela-

Your sense of humor is one of the most powerful tools you have to make certain that your daily mood and emotional state support good health.
Paul E. McGhee

tional, followed by workplace stress and an endless list of other maladies. As Gilda Radner once said, "It's always something!" All the more reason to surround ourselves with comedy, buy a joke book and memorize all the witticisms, or if all else fails, find an athletic little dog and teach it to tap-dance. Life is too serious to take seriously. Let's dub ourselves Sir—or Lady—Laughsalot!

Three Good Legs

Everyone has obstacles in life. No one, not even the rich and famous, can escape heartaches, setbacks, and disappointments. Accidents happen. Our bodies are fragile and easily broken. We simply cannot pin our happiness on being problem-free. Instead, we must overcome the obstacles we find in our path by finding ways around them. Big Red is a remarkable dog who did just that.

The particulars of Big Red's pedigree are a mystery. Some would say he's just another farm dog. He's big, though, and his looks suggest the possible presence of several breeds: German shepherd, Labrador, maybe some Irish Setter or golden retriever. In any case, his ample coat has a distinct reddish hue.

Big Red lives with sisters Ilene and Maddie in a neighborhood north of Kansas City. The sisters worked their father's farm after their parents passed away, but at the ages of sixty and sixty-two, they made the decision to sell. The physical and financial demands of running a working farm had become too much. They purchased a small home three blocks from where their younger sister, Carol, lived, and they sold the farm equipment, house, and barn at auction. Family heirlooms were passed out to sisters and brothers, nieces and nephews, and a small U-haul truck was rented to carry their personal belongings and the few pieces of furniture they needed to their new residence.

History has demonstrated that the most notable winners usually encountered heartbreaking obstacles before they triumphed. They won because they refused to become discouraged by their defeats.

B. C. Forbes

The sisters didn't take much of their old life with them. But both agreed there was one "largish" item they could not leave behind—Big Red.

He was eight years old when the sisters moved to KC. They knew it would be as big an adjustment for him as it would be for them, but they couldn't imagine giving him away or leaving him behind. Besides, they knew that Big Red had overcome greater challenges in his life. They had faith in his good nature and resilience.

As a young dog, Big Red had one disturbing flaw. He loved to chase cars and trucks. Ilene and Maddie knew this was an especially common behavior for herding breeds. Unfortunately, everything they did to try to break him of the dangerous habit failed. Then one day, what they imagined might happen did. Big Red ran after a large pickup truck and got too close. The back wheel caught one of his legs. The driver helped Ilene and Maddie get the injured dog into the back of his truck to the vet. But the news wasn't good. There was no way to save Big Red's hind leg. It was crushed.

A week after the surgery to remove his back leg, the sisters brought Big Red home and placed him on a comforter in the corner of the kitchen. They weren't sure how the sweet animal would accept his new disability. They wondered if he would become angry and mean or perhaps despondent. Only one thing was certain: Big Red's car-chasing career was over.

> *We often suffer, but we are never crushed. Even when we don't know what to do, we never give up.*
> 2 Corinthians 4:8 CEV

Big Red took his time healing, but eventually he began to push up onto his three good legs. Once on his feet, he would just stand there before finally collapsing back onto the comforter. Then one morning, Big Red took one cautious step forward, made a little hop with his one good back leg, and actually made it a few feet. The sisters, who were standing by eager to help but helpless to do so, gave him a hearty ovation. In the days ahead, Big Red conquered the three-legged walk, trotting around the yard as if he'd been born with three rather than four legs.

Ilene and Maddie were pleased to see that their favorite dog did not become mean and angry. Instead, they felt he was a sweeter animal after the accident than before, more affectionate and patient.

*Humans have external-
ized their wisdom—
stored it in museums,
libraries, the expertise
of the learned. Dog
wisdom is inside the
blood and bones.*
Donald McCaig

No one knows what tomorrow will bring. What we can decide now is that we will not let our troubles get us down, regardless of whether they are the result of our actions, the actions of others, or just dumb luck. No matter how big our challenges, God will help us adjust to a new normal and get back to making the most of our lives, just as he helped Big Red.

The Good Samaritan

The first question which the priest and the Levite asked was: "If I stop to help this man, what will happen to me?" But . . . the Good Samaritan reversed the question: "If I do not stop to help this man, what will happen to him?"
Martin Luther King Jr.

Some people instinctively put the needs of others above their own. They don't stop to think about the danger or wonder what it will cost them. They simply act. These are the people we want nearby if we should ever find ourselves in trouble far from home, trapped in a burning car, unable to defend ourselves, or alone and frightened. One such person did all she could for a precious dog named Jojo.

Jojo was a stray. He favored the area, knew some of the people who were kind enough to throw him their scraps, and played with the neighborhood kids. But by any standard, he was homeless, on his own, a dog without means. The golden retriever was plenty street-wise. He knew how to cross the road and defend himself against bigger dogs and other predators. But on this day, his personal resolve and independence failed him as he lay helpless and bleeding on the side of a rural dirt road.

The pickup truck that had come barreling down on him from behind never stopped. Either the driver didn't realize what had happened or didn't care. Perhaps he speculated, "What's another stray, give or take?" as he continued on his way. And maybe most people would have agreed with him. It's not as if someone's property had been destroyed. Some might even say that stray dogs are nothing but a public nuisance anyway.

> *Compassion, in which all ethics must take root, can only attain its full breadth and depth if it embraces all living creatures and does not limit itself to mankind.*
> Albert Schweitzer

It's impossible to know how long Jojo lay on the side of the road. What we do know is that a woman named Jeanie spotted him about two in the afternoon. She had been in the area helping an elderly friend replace a screen in her front window and measure out her medications for the week. By the time she happened along, Jojo was covered with dust and failing fast.

Jeanie threw a blanket over the middle seat of her minivan and struggled to move the injured dog. But Jojo was hurt too badly to help her. He was dead weight, and Jeanie was not a big woman. Finally, she wrapped him in the blanket, pulled him to the side of the van, and after three tries managed to get him up and inside. It wasn't ideal, but it was the best she could do. Before closing the van door, she stroked Jojo's head and reassured him that she would do everything possible to help him.

Jeanie drove to the animal hospital as quickly as she could. On the way, she kept looking back to see how the dog was doing. No movement. Considering the likelihood that she might not be able to get help for him in time started the tears flowing. Eight point three miles later, she pulled into the parking lot and ran inside to summon an attendant.

> *The King will say, "I'm telling the solemn truth: Whenever you did one of these things to someone overlooked or ignored, that was me—you did it to me."* Matthew 25:40 MSG

It seemed to her that it was hours before the vet came out to deliver an assessment of Jojo's injuries. Once he did, she wished he hadn't. Jojo's situation was dire. His right front leg was broken in three places, and his shoulder bone had a bad fracture. But that wasn't the worst of it; Jojo had life-threatening internal injuries. Surgery was needed, and the doctor warned her it would be pricey.

"Sure you want to do this?" he asked. "This could run upward of thirteen hundred dollars, and he's not even your dog. I have to tell you, too, even with the surgery, there's no guarantee he'll make it. There's another option," he continued. "One little shot, and he'd be free of his suffering."

Jeanie never hesitated. "He seems like a fighter to me," she answered. "I'll take care of the fee. Just do everything you can to save him." Three weeks later, Jojo (the name Jeanie gave him because he was a double joy) was ready to leave the hospital. But where does a homeless dog go to heal? Once again, Jeanie was sure of her answer. Jojo was going home with her.

I expect to pass through life but once. If therefore, there be any kindness I can show, or any good thing I can do to any fellow being, let me do it now, and not defer or neglect it, as I shall not pass this way again.
William Penn

As Jojo might tell us—if he could talk—at some point in our lives, we all need a Good Samaritan. Someone who will pick us up, no questions asked, and help us get back on our feet. And it's almost certain that one day when we least expect it, we will be given the opportunity to be a Good Samaritan.

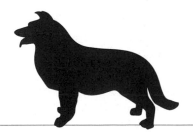

It did not take Man long . . . to discover that all the animals except the dog were impossible around the house. One has but to spend a few days with an aardvark or a llama, command a water buffalo to sit up and beg, or try to housebreak a moose, to perceive how wisely Man set about his process of elimination and selection.

James Thurber

Bonnie and Clyde

Sometimes our light goes out but is blown into flame by another human being. Each of us owes deepest thanks to those who have rekindled this light.
Albert Schweitzer

We sometimes find ourselves in unexpected situations, feeling lost and alone, unable to cope. Then a spouse, friend, sister, or brother, occasionally even a stranger, comes and stands alongside us. The situation hasn't changed, but our response has because someone is facing it with us. In that other person we find strength, comfort, and courage, enough to pull us through. We weren't meant to walk alone. We need one another.

When two black-and-white border collies were spotted walking unusually close together on a country road during a thunderstorm, passersby wondered what was up. Only when someone stopped to get a better look did it become clear that one of the dogs, a male, was blind; and the other, a female, was serving as his seeing eye dog.

The two did not have collars, so they were taken in by the

143

Meadowgreen Dog Rescue Centre in Hales, England, where a home is being sought for them. After their story received television and newspaper coverage, more than five hundred prospective owners applied to adopt the simple black-and-white dogs, whom employees at the rescue center dubbed Bonnie and Clyde.

It has been determined that Clyde, approximately five years old, went blind as the result of some type of degenerative disease. There is no way of knowing if the dogs grew up together or simply met on the road, but at this point, Clyde seems obsessively attached to Bonnie, who is thought to be several years younger. When they are together, Clyde walks about so confidently that it's difficult to see that he's blind. If for some reason he is unsure where he is, he will suddenly drop behind Bonnie and put his face on her back so she can guide him. Workers at the center say he trusts her completely. All is well with Clyde unless he can no longer sense Bonnie at his side, in which case he becomes morose, lies on the floor, and refuses to move.

> *Recollect that the Almighty, who gave the dog to be companion of our pleasures and our toils, hath invested him with a nature noble and incapable of deceit.*
> Sir Walter Scott

Bonnie's attachment to Clyde seems equally strong. She takes her job as guide for her sightless companion very seriously. Every few steps, she glances behind her to be sure he is keeping up. She could easily walk away, but she prefers to stay right with him and becomes agitated and distraught when they are separated.

Border collies are a herding breed that originated along the borders of England, Wales, and Scotland. They are highly energetic, loving dogs, believed by many to be the most intelligent of all breeds. Work has been deeply ingrained in their genealogical makeup for countless generations. For that reason, they do best when they feel they have a job, a purpose in life.

Since Bonnie and Clyde were found to be in good condition overall, it is theorized that they spent the bulk of their years herding sheep or cattle on a farm or ranch in the area. No one knows how they might have become lost—and Bonnie and Clyde aren't talking—but employees at the shelter are hopeful their original owners will see the coverage and come forward to claim the two remarkable animals.

> *Two are better than one, because they have a good reward for their toil. For if they fall, one will lift up the other. . . . Again, if two lie together, they keep warm; but how can one keep warm alone? And though one might prevail against another, two will withstand one.*
> Ecclesiastes 4:9–12
> NRSV

One of the attendants at Meadowgreen stresses that wherever the two end up, they must remain together. Through their alliance, they have become much more than two lost dogs. They have regained their confidence and sense of usefulness. Clyde, the alpha dog, provides leadership for his two-dog pack. He sets the pace. Meanwhile, Bonnie provides much-needed eyes on the world for Clyde. It's her job to identify danger and keep track of the humans. They give each other purpose and hope, and their bond is primarily responsible for their survival.

I am only one, but I am one. I cannot do everything, but I can do something. And I will not let what I cannot do interfere with what I can do.
Edward Everett Hale

Bonnie and Clyde's relationship is compelling because it demonstrates the power of two. God never intended for us to walk through this life alone. We need one another. How else can God hug us and let us know we're loved, comfort us by speaking encouraging words, and challenge us to stay in the game? Our hands are his hands; our feet, his feet; our lips, his lips. When we stand together, he stands with us, and therein lies our strength.

Who's In Charge Here?

A well-trained dog will make no attempt to share your lunch. He will just make you feel so guilty that you cannot enjoy it.
Helen Thomson

Everyone answers to someone. Rich men, beautiful women, politicians, judges, dictators, all must submit to some higher authority. There are no exceptions, though many fancy themselves to be above the bounds of earthly accountability and free to do as they please without consequences. Dogs have a hierarchical system, as well. Curly is the big cheese in his doggy world—until the humans show up.

He came to us at two months, an energetic, coal black ball of curls. We, being people of extraordinary imagination, named him Curly. He was a Schnauzer/Poodle mix, what is now known as a schnoodle. Though gentle and protective with the children, Curly was quite a turf warrior. He kept a close eye on things both inside the house and out.

Outside the house, Curly was fearless. Though he did not leave the confines of our yard, he would bark loudly at any animal that passed on the street, big or small. This was not so much to warn us as it was to ensure there was no misunderstanding dog-to-dog about who ruled that particular domain. For this reason, Curly spent a good bit of time indoors.

> *A leaderless family is like a ship without a rudder and potentially disastrous when it comes to dealing with dogs, especially those who get wind in their sails.*
> Nicholas H. Dodman

Curly was probably four or five years old when Missy, whose story has already been told, took up residence in our yard and refused to leave. Curly checked her out cautiously. He must have found her sufficiently submissive, for he never challenged her presence or insisted that she leave.

Once we made the decision to keep her and brought her inside, we noticed that Curly quickly trained Missy to follow his lead. He taught her to stand and wait until he had finished at the doggy food and water dishes. If she tried to approach ahead of him, he would snap at her and stare her down. His low-pitched growl let her know where she was not allowed to sit or lie. Her compliance was nonnegotiable. Curly had first option with the humans, as well. Whenever we came into the house, Curly insisted that Missy hang back and allow him to greet us first.

It's no secret that dogs are social pack animals. At the top of the pack is a dominant or alpha dog that is in charge within the family unit. This hierarchy is an instinctive part of a dog's nature. Either the animal will submit to those who are dominant or dominate those who are submissive.

Obey your leaders and submit to their authority. They keep watch over you as men who must give an account. Obey them so that their work will be a joy, not a burden, for that would be of no advantage to you.
Hebrews 13:17 NIV

Clearly, Curly had secured his dominance over Missy. Though she was the larger dog, she was also the newcomer, the female, and the less assertive of the two. He tolerated her presence in our home because she was willing to play by his rules. In time, the two dogs became quite affectionate. Curly would position himself on the sofa or in a chair with his head near the edge. She would sit on the floor just below him.

But Curly's alpha-dog dominance did not extend to the humans in our home. We made it clear early on what behaviors were and were not considered acceptable, and our schnoodle complied.

Humans are not pack animals, but we do live within the bounds of certain social constructs that bring order and safety to our lives. For example, a teacher dominates in the classroom but must answer to the school administrator, who in turn answers to the school board. Those who dominate others by use of force will answer to law enforcement and the courts. Even dictators who have risen above the law in their own countries are often brought down by revolt or the actions of the international community.

> *A child is fortunate who is taught early in life to respect authority. Not to accept it blindly, of course, but to honor it as the construct that brings order out of chaos.*
> John Amos Fletcher

On an elemental level, Curly teaches us that we all must submit to authority in our lives. Authority is there for our good and the good of others. It keeps our human natures in check by curbing the brutality that comes with unrestrained power. The next time your boss gives you an unpleasant assignment or makes a decision you don't like, remember that he, too, answers to someone. So does the judge who rules against you and the legislator who imposes higher taxes. Everyone answers to someone.

A Matter of Life and Death

*No man is worth his salt who is
not ready at all times to risk his
body, to risk his well-being, to
risk his life, in a great cause.*
Theodore Roosevelt

Two men pull a motorist from a burning car just before it explodes. A nurse may risk contracting a deadly virus in order to care for her patients. Firefighters quickly make their way into a collapsing building. Men and women often walk a tight line between life and death in behalf of others. And nowhere is their courage more common than on the fields of battle.

Not all who valiantly go to war are of the human kind. Dogs have given their lives in combat for thousands of years. They have fought alongside Egyptians, Greeks, Persians, Britons, and Romans, and they have faithfully carried out their duties in every modern war. In Vietnam alone, these amazing war dogs and their handlers are thought to have saved at least ten thousand lives.

Ron Aiello voluntarily joined the Marine Corps and headed for

Camp Lejeune, North Carolina, in 1965. Once there, he was offered a fascinating opportunity—attending the dog training school at Fort Benning, Georgia.

After a week of classroom instruction, Ron and a couple of his buddies were given slips of paper with the names of their canine comrades. The men quickly left for the kennels, where Ron went from cage to cage until he found Stormy, an eighteen-month-old tan and black female German shepherd.

> *Animals are reliable, many full of love, true in their affections, predictable in their actions, grateful, and loyal. Difficult standard for people to live up to.*
> Alfred A. Montapert

Man and dog spent some time getting to know each other before entering a rigorous training regimen that included training for obedience, communicating verbally and with hand motions, communicating from a distance, and scouting. When they had mastered it all in the daylight, they began again, learning to do it all equally well at night. Three months later they were ready to leave for Vietnam with thirty other dog teams, part of the First Marine Scout Dog Platoon.

The flight itself took five days, and twenty more days were spent getting Stormy acclimated to the hot, muggy climate. Even when they were ready to go to work, though, it was necessary to convince doubtful field commanders who weren't sure a dog could spot a sniper in a tree or an almost invisible trip line hidden in the brush.

Ron and Stormy were one of the first teams to be called upon, and both were eager to take their training to the field. Their first assignment was to scout two villages. They found nothing of note in the first, but just before entering the second, Stormy alerted, telling Ron there was danger ahead. As trained, Ron dropped to one knee, moved up as close as possible to her, and turned his head in the direction she was looking so he could see from her vantage point. Just as he did, a sniper opened up from a nearby tree. Ron and Stormy quickly took cover behind a small embankment as the Marines moved forward and disarmed the sniper. Stormy saved Ron's life on their very first day in action.

> The LORD is my fortress, protecting me from danger, so why should I tremble? . . . Though a mighty army surrounds me, my heart will not be afraid. Even if I am attacked, I will remain confident.
>
> Psalm 27:1–3 NLT

Ron served thirteen months with Stormy. He asked for another tour with her, but he was denied. He was told that the new handler would arrive the next day, and once the hand-off was complete, he would have to leave the base. Stormy could not bond with her new handler as long as she was distracted by the previous one.

Ron left Vietnam in 1967, but Stormy stayed and worked

until at least the summer of 1970. Through the years, Ron has met three of Stormy's handlers at reunions and by e-mail.

More than four decades have passed since Ron and Stormy served together, but he still speaks of her with great emotion—their bond was and is unbreakable. During those months when life and death were just a breath apart, Ron and Stormy were together 24-7. They slept together, ate together, played together, and worked together. They watched over each other and placed their lives on the line for each other.

> *The summer soldier and the sunshine patriot will, in this crisis, shrink from the service of their country; but he that stands it now, deserves the love and thanks of man and woman.*
> Thomas Paine

Stepping forward and risking our lives for the good of others is never easy. Our human sense of self-preservation is strong. But we are capable of great courage and nobility. Many people—and canines—before us have demonstrated that. We are stronger than we think—strong enough to do the right thing.

Skin and Bones

*I hope to make people realize how totally
helpless animals are, how dependent on
us, trusting as a child must be that we
will be kind and take care of their needs.*

James Herriot

Random House Webster's Dictionary defines *domesticate:*
"to tame an animal through generations of breeding to
live in close association with human beings as a pet or
work animal, usually creating a dependency that elimi-
nates the animal's ability to live in the wild." Dogs have
been domesticated for thousands of years. We humans
stand between them and survival, and it's a responsibility we must take seriously.

The black dachshund had been their family pet, but when the
baby came along, he was relegated to the backyard. A few months
later, a neighbor came by with a brown Chihuahua she had found
on the loose. "Put her in the back," the dachshund's owner said.
"She can keep my dog company until her owner is found." A litter
of puppies resulted before the Chihuahua wriggled through a hole
in the gate and took off again for parts unknown. The puppies,

already undernourished and dehydrated, withered in the triple-digit summer temperatures. Only one puppy survived.

It isn't clear why, but things got better for the dachshund and the surviving puppy for a while. The owners gave them food and water more regularly, and they even came out in the back to play sometimes. The little puppy grew and matured.

Providing food and shelter is not proving love for your pet. Those too, but proper care and protection from harm make the truest sense of responsible pet ownership.
John D. Carraway

Less than a year passed before a second child arrived, and the relationships inside the house took a downward turn. Once again, the animals in the backyard got the worst of it. Since neither of the dogs had been spayed or neutered, another litter soon appeared near the back porch steps. There were five little wiggly, hairless bodies this time. Their mother did her best, but she was helpless to care for them in the heat of summer with so little to eat and drink herself. The smallest died within a week. A month later, two more died. The two surviving puppies, a speckled mix and a thin black one, hung on tenaciously.

Neighbors who noticed the plight of the dogs pleaded with the animals' owner to do something, but she insisted that everything was under control. Neighbors ran a hose under the fence and poured dog food on the ground where the animals could reach it, but the owner saw what they had done and ordered them to leave her dogs alone. Neighbors asked for weeks to let them find homes for the puppies, and even offered to pay for them. "I'm saving those dogs for my kids," she protested.

The authorities finally were called, and a police officer came by to look. He noted the obvious signs of neglect and promised that someone would follow up, but no one did. The situation looked hopeless until one day the two little pups found their way through the hole in the gate and into the yard next door. Like desperate prisoners who had somehow managed to elude the guards and breach the wall, they waddled their way to freedom.

> *The godly care for their animals, but the wicked are always cruel.*
> Proverbs 12:10 NLT

Seeing their determination to live, the neighbors took them in out of the heat and gave them food, water, and a safe place to rest. Dubbed Skin and Bones by their rescuers, the little dogs managed to show their appreciation by licking their hands and eating everything in sight. Things were going well, but the rescuers quickly realized the pups were still endangered in their emaciated state. They called a local rescue group and heard what they were hoping to hear. Taking even an endangered dog from someone else's yard is a felony, but since they found the animals wandering "at large" on their property, they had every right and obligation to turn them over to the shelter. Once in their custody, the pups would be lovingly nursed back to health by trained staff members under the supervision of a veterinarian and later placed in responsible homes.

> *Never doubt that a small group of concerned citizens can change the world. Indeed, it's the only thing that ever has.*
> Margaret Mead

A few days later, the authorities finally followed up on the adult dogs, and they, too, were taken to safety. The owners received a citation with a steep fine attached.

The story of Skin and Bones, part tragedy and part jubilation, reminds us that animals cannot be regarded as toys or possessions. Along with their cute little faces, wiggly bodies, and wagging tails comes a sober responsibility. They are completely dependent on us for their very survival, and to let them down is simply unacceptable.

Where There's Smoke, There's Fire

Every happening, great and small, is a parable whereby God speaks to us, and the art of life is to get the message.
Malcolm Muggeridge

Almost everyone can recall a situation where they felt trapped into doing something they didn't want to do, only to find that it became a great blessing to them. Apparently, we humans don't always know what we want or what we need. But God does, and he often answers prayers that we haven't prayed—prayers that we might one morning wake up to thank him for.

"This has been our home for twenty-two years." That's how Diane's interview with the newspaper reporter began. "We've had many holiday dinners and birthday parties here, many memories. It's hard to believe it's gone." Diane swallowed hard to hold back the tears. "At least we got out—and that's all on account of Maggie."

During the wee hours of a nippy October morning, the house at 1465 Anise Street burned. What the flames missed, the smoke and water ruined. It was a mess. Hours after the fire was extinguished, the smell of smoke and melted plastic lingered in the air and a puddle of water clung to the curb in the street out front. Diane, fifty-seven, and her mother, Agnes, seventy-nine, watched the firefighters do their jobs from the yard across the street. Their five-year-old Irish Setter, Maggie, stood between them as if to ensure that neither of the women would suddenly dash across the street and back into harm's way. Diane and Agnes were still in their nightclothes, with blankets provided by the paramedics pulled tightly around their shoulders, when the reporter approached them. Diane really didn't feel like talking, but she was eager to give Maggie the credit she deserved.

A wise Dog Person once described a perfect world as one in which every dog would have a home, and every home would have a dog.
Mary Tiegreen

Around eight in the morning, a kindhearted neighbor offered them temporary refuge in her home. Agnes went to sleep in a back bedroom, and Diane sat alone in the borrowed living room. She stared out the window at the mess across the street. Just a few hours earlier she had been sleeping soundly in her own bed with Maggie at her feet. She reached down and stroked the top of the dog's head. They were both exhausted.

Diane had hit the roof when her nineteen-year-old son, Troy, arrived home from college one weekend with a dog he'd picked up on the highway. "I was maybe twenty or thirty miles out of Nacogdoches when I saw her," he told his mom. "She's a great-looking dog, and I figured she had to belong to someone, but there wasn't any ID. I couldn't just leave her there! I think we should call her Maggie."

If we don't know how or what to pray, it doesn't matter. He does our praying in and for us, making prayer out of our wordless sighs, our aching groans. He knows us far better than we know ourselves.
Romans 8:26–27 MSG

"You mean I should call her Maggie, since you'll be going back to school tomorrow," Diane answered.

Troy's "Yeah, I guess" said it all.

Diane had never owned a dog, and she was sure she didn't want the trouble. But the tall Irish Setter with a mahogany coat and lively hazel eyes was hard to resist. It wasn't as if she could ask Troy to take her back to where he found her. Like it or not, she would have to make the best of it.

Three months later, Maggie had gained Diane's respect. She stayed with Agnes when Diane was at work, and both women felt safer with Maggie around. She was easy to care for, was always grateful, and provided an unexpected source of affection. Then on the morning of the fire, Maggie proved to be a lifesaver. She nudged and barked at Diane, not just once but repeatedly. Diane finally had no choice but to get up and see why her usually well-behaved dog was jumping up onto the bed, pulling at her hand and growling. Maggie led Diane out of the bedroom and down the smoky hallway to Agnes's room. From there, she led the two women, now fully aware of the catastrophe, through the smoke to the front door.

> *Whenever I see sunbeams coming through clouds, it always looks to me like God shining himself down onto us. The thing about sunbeams is they're always there even though we can't always see them. Same with God.*
> Adeline Cullen Ray

Today Diane's home has been restored, something she hadn't imagined was possible on that eventful October morning. Maggie, however, is gone, reclaimed by her family, who read the newspaper article and recognized their heroic missing pet. Diane and Agnes aren't alone, though. Maggie's puppy, Jill, is now living with them.

Under no circumstances would Diane have prayed for a dog. She had never had one and never intended to. And yet her mother's life and her own were saved by the diligence and resourcefulness of a remarkable animal.

The Legend of TJ

*We are not the same persons this year
as last; nor are those we love. It is a
happy chance if we, changing, continue
to love a changed person.*
William Somerset Maugham

Just as people grow and mature, so do their relationships. Ask two people who have been married fifty years if their relationship looks and feels the same on their anniversary day as it did on their wedding day. That doesn't mean their love for each other has lessened, only that their relationship has changed as they have changed as people. In fact, the strength of any long-term relationship is the willingness to accommodate those changes.

When Greg, a dogcatcher, spotted the young black mutt with gray beard and chest hair, the dog was—as they say in the animal-control biz—at large. Greg followed the pup for a block or so before cornering him in a cul-de-sac. For a moment, man and dog faced off, and then the dog closed the distance between them, tail wagging and brown eyes flashing a greeting as warm as a hug.

Greg found the animal so charming that he let him ride in the front of the truck with him that day—and the day after that, and the day after that. In Houston or Seattle such an action might have

> *Did you ever notice when you blow in a dog's face he gets mad at you? But when you take him in a car he sticks his head out the window.*
>
> Steve Bluestone

been considered a serious breach of animal-control protocol, but in little old out-of-the-way Buffalo, Wyoming, no one questioned it, except to say, "Hey, Greg, where'd you get the cool dog?"

One day Greg saw a high school kid he knew out for a run. He followed in the truck until the kid stopped for a rest. "Hey, Todd, you gotta see this dog I found," he told him. "He likes to run—just like you! What a coincidence. And the crazy thing is, he's looking for a home."

The high school kid's mother had one condition when she saw him running up the front walk with the black mutt at his side. "No way that animal comes in here until you get him thoroughly checked out." Figuring that her declaration held an implied "Yes, you can keep him," Todd took the mutt over to the vet's office. The doc said the dog was about a year old, probably had some black Lab, border collie, and English shepherd in him, and seemed to be in good shape. That night Todd and his brothers settled on a name—TJ (short for Tom Jackson, a linebacker on their revered Denver Broncos football team).

Todd soon realized that the dogcatcher was right about TJ. He could run forever, all fifty pounds of lean dog flesh keeping pace mile after mile. The two were well-matched running partners throughout Todd's high school, college, and early adult years, routinely running ten miles or more a day. Todd's father, and perhaps a significant number of Buffalo's residents, referred to the duo as "a couple of running fools"!

But as TJ approached his ninth year, Todd noticed he wasn't keeping up quite as well. Todd intentionally took him on shorter runs, stopped more often for a drink at the water fountain on their route, and slowed the pace out of consideration for the dog's aging muscles and joints. Todd also began to give him other types of attention. They spent a lot more time just hanging out, and they went for long rides in the car with TJ hanging his head out the window taking in the breeze. Some family members even intimated that Todd liked to take TJ along on his dates.

Above all, maintain constant love for one another, for love covers a multitude of sins. Be hospitable to one another without complaining. Like good stewards of the manifold grace of God, serve one another with whatever gift each of you has received.
1 Peter 4:8–10 NRSV

By late in TJ's tenth year, he could barely walk. Arthritic joints limited him to walking around the porch. Going up and down stairs was painful. Todd was a busy man by then, living on his own, but he still had time for his old running partner. They would sit on the shady porch and reminisce about old times—though Todd did all the talking. Their relationship had certainly changed since the black mutt and the high school kid first ran like the wind together, but their love for each other had only grown stronger. There was a gentleness about it, a love centered on familiarity, trust, and caring.

> *It seems to me that the best relationships — the ones that last — are frequently the ones that are rooted in friendship. You know, one day you look at the person and you see something more than you did the night before.*
> Gillian Anderson

Our human relationships are constantly changing, as well. Those who succeed in relationships exhibit a mutual willingness to take what they have to the next level. They allow their relationships to grow, evolve, and reinvent themselves over time.

Quantum Leaps

People think responsibility is hard to bear.
It's not. I think that sometimes it is the
absence of responsibility that is harder to
bear. You have a great feeling of impotence.
Henry Kissinger

When we see people we love struggling, it's natural to try to help by excusing them from their obligations and lightening their load. If the struggle is about overwork or worry, this is an effective strategy. But when the issue is self-esteem, the opposite is often true. For the struggling person, honoring a commitment, caring for another's needs, and doing a good job promote self-esteem. Accomplishment becomes a cherished ego boost.

Mandy is a beautiful teenage girl with auburn hair, hazel eyes, and a porcelain complexion. She's exceptionally bright, kind, and caring and is a wonderful daughter. But her sweet, unassuming smile masked a heart of painful insecurity. Despite all she had going for her, Mandy felt worthless. She saw herself as a noncontributor, with nothing to offer her friends and family or the world at large.

Mandy's timidity and lack of confidence made her the brunt of jokes and the victim of bullies, further impairing her inner vision of herself. She was at an age when most teenagers struggle with self-esteem, but Mandy's low self-esteem was chronic. She had begun acting out in ways that concerned her parents. They tried to ease her stress by backing off chores and going easy on her for missed school assignments, but things seemed to be getting worse rather than better.

The trouble with having a dog is that you have to take care of it—that is also the wonderful thing about having a dog.
Trudy Truman

At the urging of their pastor, Mandy's parents went with her to a counselor who specializes in issues common to young adults. The first visit was spent warming up to each other and touching on the basics. On the second visit, the counselor began to expound on the virtues of dog ownership. Mandy's parents, who were asked to attend her early sessions, rolled their eyes and exchanged glances. They'd had dogs before, and they knew what a bother they could be. Now, with four children, busy schedules, and Mandy's emotional needs vying for attention, the idea of adding a dog to the mix seemed ludicrous. The counselor was persistent, however. The dog would not be a family pet. It would be Mandy's dog, her responsibility alone.

It took a week or two for Mandy's parents to come to terms

with the idea, but finally they agreed to try the get-a-dog approach and began looking for a suitable candidate for Mandy. They didn't have to look far. They remembered a couple in the church who had recently announced they were looking for a good home for their precious Chelsee. They had to kennel the dog far too frequently in order to tend to ailing parents in another city. A phone call and brief visit later, a deal was struck.

What are human beings that you are mindful of them, mortals that you care for them? Yet you have made them a little lower than God, and crowned them with glory and honor. You have given them dominion over the works of your hands.
Psalm 8:4–6 NRSV

Chelsee was beautiful—a two-year-old Gordon Setter with a long, silky black coat and copper-colored dots for eyebrows. She bonded immediately with Mandy. Like most Gordon Setters, Chelsee is extraordinarily loving and loyal. She now sleeps in Mandy's bed at night and has become her constant companion. But Gordon Setters are also known to be stubborn and demanding. They aren't easy to train, and they need to be walked a minimum of a mile a day. They are a taxing responsibility for any dog owner.

Along with the usual task of keeping the food and water bowls replenished, Mandy must spend more than an hour a week combing out Chelsee's long coat and giving her a bath when needed.

Mandy gets up to take her out, even if it's in the middle of the night, applies her flea and tick treatments, schedules and takes her to vet visits, and makes sure she gets the exercise she craves. Chelsee repays her generously by snuggling up close to her while they watch a movie and sitting quietly at her feet while she does her schoolwork. Mandy has even taken on a small job. She and Chelsee walk the neighbors' dogs before the owners get home from work in the evening.

> *We do not believe in ourselves until someone reveals that deep inside us something is valuable, worth listening to, worthy of our trust, sacred to our touch.*
> E. E. Cummings

Mandy's parents thought Chelsee might be too much responsibility for her, but Mandy took to the challenge with passion and determination. Carrying the responsibility for another living thing boosted her confidence and sense of worth. Mandy is starting to think differently about herself. Her doctor says she's made quantum leaps forward.

God has put within each of us a need to be needed. Taking care of Chelsee gave Mandy the purpose she was lacking and the acceptance she needed to heal.

Forgive and Forget

I've had a few arguments with people, but I never carry a grudge. You know why? While you're carrying a grudge, they're out dancing.
Buddy Hackett

God has assured us that he not only forgives us but he distances himself from the offense so that it will never affect our relationship with him again. He urges us to follow his example and do the same for those who hurt and offend us. It's a God-sized task, something we can do only with his help and a willingness to try. Perhaps a Schnauzer with a long memory can teach us how to let go of those grudges.

Karen's grandmother calls Schnauzers "children in fur coats." They are playful and loyal, bright and sassy, and often all too prone to mischief. They also have incredible memories. If you get one mad at you, she'll hold a grudge forever.

Sadie was purchased from a breeder in Texas and named for Karen's grandmother's best friend. The first time the two met,

Sadie jumped right up into Karen's lap, pushed her backward in the chair, and stared into her eyes. Karen had done some research on the breed, but she quickly realized this particular Schnauzer would greatly exceed her expectations.

Karen was working very long hours establishing a new law office, and she got into the habit of taking Sadie to the office with her. She actually did well there under Karen's watchful eye. She was quiet, respectful, and a real charmer with the clients. Karen's assistant came to think of her as her "granddog."

> *Somewhere my doggie pulls and tugs the fringes of rebellious rugs, or with the mischief of a pup chews all of my shoes and slippers up. And when he's done it to the core with eyes all eager, pleads for more.*
> John Kendrick Bangs

At home, Sadie was more demonstrative. She liked to run through the house, flinging her stuffed animals in the air and catching them again. It turned out she was an excellent mouser and loved to deposit her catches at Karen's feet. Sadie seemed to have an incredibly accurate sense of time. She always seemed to know when to hop up on the sofa and watch from the window as the neighbors walked past with their two Shih Tzus at precisely five in the afternoon. And she was obsessed with bedtime. At nine every evening, she would present herself to Karen and bark, signaling that it was time to head for bed. If Karen failed to respond, she would get a play toy and begin to bang it on Karen's leg. Each time she was rebuffed, Sadie would up the ante until Karen would give up and turn in for the night.

When Sadie was about a year old, Karen decided it was time for some obedience training. On several occasions, Sadie had gotten away from her in the yard and refused to come when called. "This one has a mind of her own," Karen told her brother. Hewitt had seen a good bit of success training his own dogs and offered to help. He was sure little Sadie would be a piece of cake. He was wrong.

First Hew put Sadie on an eight-foot lead, called her, and tugged gently for Sadie to come. Nothing. The Schnauzer wouldn't budge. She wouldn't even look his way. After a

As high as heaven is over the earth, so strong is his love to those who fear him. And as far as sunrise is from sunset, he has separated us from our sins.
Psalm 103:11–12 MSG

half hour, he threw up his hands and said he would return the following evening. Hew arrived for a second try with a twenty-five-foot lead, thinking this would give Sadie a greater sense of freedom and the feeling that she could move in the right direction without giving in completely. Karen intervened after an hour as Hew was threatening to pull the stubborn little animal across the yard "the hard way!"

The interesting thing is that Sadie never forgot. She holds a grudge against Hew to this day. Fourteen long months later, Sadie was sitting on Karen's lap at a family reunion when Hew walked in the door. The minute she saw him, Sadie began to growl in a low, menacing voice. A year later, Karen and Sadie were asleep at her family's summer home in New Mexico. At one in the morning, Hew came quietly in the front door, and Sadie stood on the end of Karen's bed and growled.

> *"I can forgive, but I cannot forget" is only another way of saying, "I will not forgive." Forgiveness ought to be like a canceled note — torn in two and burned up so that it never can be shown against one.*
> Paul Boese

Some human grudges can put Schnauzer grudges to shame, however. They've been known to separate families, break up marriages, and destroy long-standing friendships. They are never productive because each time the offended remembers the offense, he or she is wounded again. Like Sadie, we may not have the capacity to actually forget; but like God, we can distance ourselves from the offense so that it doesn't continue to hurt us.

It is by muteness that a dog becomes for one so utterly beyond value; with him one is at peace where words play no torturing tricks. When he just sits lovingly and knows that he is being loved, those are the moments that I think are precious to a dog; when, with his adoring soul coming through his eyes, he feels that you are really thinking of him.

John Galsworthy